KING'S QUEST

MASK OF ETERNITY™

Prima's Official Strategy Guide

Rick Barba

Prima Publishing
Rocklin, California
(916) 632-4400
www.primagames.com

Project Editor: Sara E. Wilson

Important:
Prima Publishing has made every effort to determine that the information contained in this book is accurate. However, the publisher makes no warranty, either expressed or implied, as to the accuracy, effectiveness, or completeness of the material in this book; nor does the publisher assume liability for damages, either incidental or consequential, that may result from using the information in this book. The publisher cannot provide information regarding game play, hints and strategies, or problems with hardware or software. Questions should be directed to the support numbers provided by the game and device manufacturers in their documentation. Some game tricks require precise timing and may require repeated attempts before the desired result is achieved.

ISBN: 7615-1115-6
Library of Congress Catalog Card Number: 97-68845
Printed in the United States of America

98 99 00 01 II 9 8 7 6 5 4 3 2 1

Contents

Contents

Contents

Introduction

Welcome to the official strategy guide for *King's Quest: Mask of Eternity*, the most revolutionary development in graphic adventure gaming since—well, since the original *King's Quest* essentially established the genre back in 1984.

In fact, calling *Mask of Eternity* a "graphic adventure" seems almost retrogressive, sort of like calling a Ferrari Testarossa a "motor car." With its stunning use of 3-D technology, *Mask of Eternity* features the most seamless integration of storytelling, character, immersive action, and puzzle-solving I've ever seen in a computer game.

HOW TO USE THIS BOOK

This guide couldn't be easier to use. Note, however, that it is not a substitute for the *King's Quest: Mask of Eternity* game manual. As a "strategy guide," this book assumes you've read the manual and are familiar with the *Mask of Eternity* interface. If this is not the case— well, please go away now and read the game documentation. Don't worry, the next paragraph will wait for you. Really, it's got all day.

This *Mask of Eternity* annotated walkthrough is a detailed, step-by-step solution path through the game. The walkthrough is divided into seven chapters, one for each of the seven fantastical regions in *Mask of Eternity*. Use the table of contents or the index to find the location or puzzle perplexing you, and then turn to that section to get all the answers you seek.

What does "annotated" mean, exactly? In this case, it means you get more than just quick, mindless solutions. You get explanations of plot and/or puzzle logic; you get background information; you may even get a few inside notes on the game design.

Here's a short sample illustrating how an annotated walkthrough works:

Name of Location/Puzzle

Sometimes locations or puzzles need a setup or description. In the *Mask of Eternity* annotated walkthrough, a few short sentences usually introduce each new venue.

- Then comes a list of "action bullet points."

- These are tasks you must complete to win the game.

- Or, in some cases, a bullet point denotes an optional, fun thing to try.

- In any case, you can skip the annotation and simply refer to the action bullet points, if you want.

But sometimes, adventure gamers want more than just answers. They want *explanations*. So you'll find background information, author commentary, discussion of plot or puzzle logic, and other incidental material in paragraphs like this, tucked between the action bullet points.

- More action bullet points follow.

- Task after task is clearly and concisely spelled out.

- Eventually, you win the game.

- Life pales to normal again.

- You start checking the Sierra website, looking for word of *King's Quest IX*.

Introduction

One last note about this book's walkthrough: It's not by any means the only path through this game. *Mask of Eternity* tells a basically linear story. But the game's three-dimensional universe lets you, the player, "tell" that story in myriad ways. This walkthrough, based on the designers' own optimal solution path, tries to tell the story efficiently without sacrificing dramatic effect.

Enjoy.

CHAPTER 1
Kingdom of Daventry

elcome to Daventry, the heart of the King's Quest universe. Connor starts in front of neighbor Sarah's house. That raven perched atop the petrified Sarah seems to be squawking with a purpose, doesn't it? Before you deal with the bird, enter Sarah's house and take a look around.

Figure 1-1
Nevermore? The bird wants something, apparently. Shoo it off Sarah's stone head, and then watch where it flies.

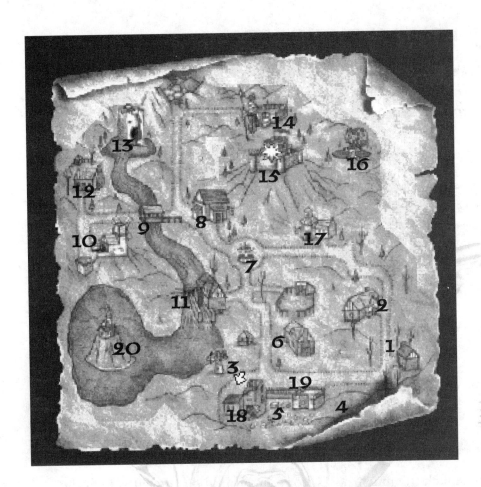

1. Start (Sarah's House)
2. Connor's House
3. Wizard
4. Cliff (to Mausoleum Roof)
5. Graveyard
6. Simms's Farmhouse
7. Town Fountain
8. Tavern
9. Bridge
10. Windmill
11. Mill
12. Kavanagh's House
13. Waterfall
14. Tomb of Sir James
15. Castlekeep Ruins (Teleport)
16. Beast/Unicorn
17. Alchemist's House
18. Church
19. Mausoleum
20. Wizard's House

SARAH'S HOUSE (INTERIOR)

Sarah's mother, the Widow Burke, stands stone-cold in the middle of the room. What vile curse sits astride the fair land of Daventry? (Sorry, I'm starting to write like Connor talks.)

> **Tip**
>
> Don't click on the kettle near the fire in Sarah's house unless your red Health meter is low. It holds a serving of warm, health-giving broth. If you drink the broth with a full Health rating, you waste it.

- Grab the five mushrooms from the basket on the table.
- Get the Potion of Shield from the shelf between the two beds.
- Exit the house.

SARAH'S HOUSE (EXTERIOR)

- Pluck the mushrooms from the ground on the left side of the house.
- A lumbering Goblin loiters on the right side of the house. Click on your Hand Weapon—in this case, your fists—in the bar at the bottom of the screen.
- Punch out the Goblin and search its body for mushrooms or other items.
- Look for a pile of coins tucked in a small corner on the side of the house.

Figure 1-2
Good Fungus. Keep a sharp eye out for mushrooms. Pick them now, eat them later to boost your health.

Figure 1-3
First Fight. Do a Holyfield on this Goblin and loot its foul corpse. Who said heroism isn't fun?

Tip

If your Health suffers in the Goblin fight—and it probably will in this, your first fight—go back inside Sarah's house and drink from the soup kettle *before* you pop mushrooms.

Click on the raven and watch it fly off down the road. Hmmm . . . whither does it fly?

Don't follow it yet. First, turn right on the road and follow it to the next house.

CONNOR'S HOUSE (EXTERIOR)

Punch the bull's-eye target in the field until your Experience rating rises. (It rises only once.)

Punch the bull's-eye target in the enclosed side yard until your Experience rises. (Again, it rises only once.)

Pick the trio of mushrooms growing on the lawn left of the entryway. Watch for a roving Goblin; avoid it for now.

Open the door, and then enter the house.

Figure 1-4
Home Sweet Home.
Yes, this is your pad.
Note the tasteful
bull's-eye motif.

CHAPTER 1 Kingdom of Daventry　　　**7**

CONNOR'S HOUSE (INTERIOR)

When Connor enters his home, the raven returns and camps on the fence post across the road, cawing in a most irritating manner. We'll give it attention in a moment. First, let's gather a few necessary items.

- Walk into the back room.
- Grab the dagger stuck in the tabletop. Finally, a weapon!
- If your Health meter is low, take a sip of the stuff simmering in the kettle by the fire.
- Click on the cookie jar on the bottom shelf in the corner to open it.
- Take the 35 gold coins.
- Exit the house.

Figure 1-5 **Savings Withdrawal.** Yes, Connor, this is the rainy day you've been saving for. *Raid that cookie jar!*

CONNOR'S HOUSE (EXTERIOR)

- If you haven't already, battle the Goblin near your house. (It will be *much* easier with the dagger.)
- Click on the raven sitting on the fence post. Watch him fly away again.
- Follow the bird down the road this time.
- Take the road past Sarah's house, and then down the hill to the right. Look for the mausoleum and church, the next buildings on the left side of the road.

caution

Watch out for the Spriggan shooting crossbow bolts at you from the church graveyard! (It's the fenced area between the mausoleum and the church.) You can't reach him from here, so go past on the far-right side of the road.

THE LAKE AND WIZARD

- Run past the churchyard area to the lakeshore, where the Wizard shouts, "Come closer, lad!"
- Dispose of the Goblin staggering around the shore.
- Click on the Wizard to talk to him.

The Wizard explains the calamity that has befallen Daventry. Five fragments of the Mask of Eternity were scattered across the land by a magical tempest conjured by an evil entity. Connor now possesses one fragment; thus, only four remain. Your quest: Find the remaining four pieces of the Mask, and then return the Mask to its most holy sanctuary.

Figure 1-6
Half Stoned. The Wizard avoided total petrification, but his mobility is a tad hindered. Fortunately, he still has his wits—and a magic map for you.

Finally, the Wizard conjures you a magic map, a handy tool for hero adventurers. You can access this map anytime by pressing Tab.

- Go back up the hill toward Sarah's house. Remember to stay on the far side of the road from the churchyard to avoid the Spriggan's crossbow bolts.

Figure 1-7
Long Jump. Take a running leap from the cliff to the top of the mausoleum.

Near the top of the hill, veer right and double back across the rock plateau to the cliff overlooking the mausoleum. (Connor notes the long jump, but he can make it.)

CHURCHYARD (MAUSOLEUM)

Save your game here!

Make a running jump from the cliff to the mausoleum roof.

Arm yourself with the dagger.

Proceed to the opening at the far end of the roof.

When the camera angle changes, step forward. Connor automatically jumps down and dispatches the Spriggan most efficiently. Cool!

Grab the crossbow dropped by the Spriggan.

Figure 1-8
Ambush. Drop onto the Spriggan from above. You lose an enemy and gain a crossbow.

caution

Be quick in the graveyard! Even on Easy Combat setting, these rising Zombies are tough enemies, given your weapons and experience at this point. Unless your Experience rating is at least 5, you may not be ready to deal with them just yet.

- Try the mausoleum door if you want. It's barred, and you can't break in yet.

- Run! Moaning Zombies rise from the graveyard, so sprint around the mausoleum to the road.

- Go to the farmhouse just across the road.

FARMER SIMMS'S HOUSE

- Enter the farmhouse.

- Help yourself to the mushrooms in the basket on the table.

- Take the leather boots next to the bed. Connor dons them automatically, and your Armor rating rises a point.

- Take the coins from the shelf.

- Open the small chest on the shelf and take 25 more coins.

- Exit the house.

SIMMS'S FARMYARD

 Tip For some grisly fun, take crossbow target practice on the chickens in the farmyard.

- Turn right and go around the house.

- A monster lurks near the petrified Farmer Simms. Kill and loot it.

- If you go behind the farmhouse, a pair of Zombies rises from the ground. Kill and loot them.

- Go to the farm stand directly across the road from the farmhouse.

FARM STAND/FOUNTAIN

- Empty all three baskets of mushrooms into your inventory. If you need a health boost, eat the fish and fowl hanging in the stand.

- Go north up the road to the fountain and take a good draught, if you need a bit of health. (Which way is north? Check your map to see.)

- Continue northwest up the road to the tavern.

TAVERN

- Go behind the bar counter.

- Take the leather gloves near Julia, the petrified bartender. Connor dons them automatically and gains another point in his Armor rating.

- Raid the small chest on the shelf of its gold coins. Julia won't mind.

- For fun, take a few sips from the ale mugs scattered about.

- Go upstairs to the balcony.

- Open the large chest and take the Healing Crystals.

- Exit the tavern.

- Use any weapon to shatter the two barrels on the west side of the tavern. Both contain health items.

Figure 1-9
Crystal Health. Don't forget to raid the chest in the tavern balcony. These crystals have excellent healing properties.

THE BRIDGE

From the tavern, head west to the bridge. As you approach, watch for a very tough, active Spriggan. Take him down from afar with the crossbow, if you can.

Cross the bridge.

At the Kavanagh house, turn left (south) and take a few steps up the road to the windmill.

WINDMILL (EXTERIOR)

Look up to see the windmill. Anybody home?

Kill the two vicious hopping Spriggans who await your arrival.

Figure 1-10
The Windmill. Get ready for some serious combat in and around this high Daventry landmark.

How? One Spriggan is bad enough, but two are deadly. Fire as many crossbow bolts as possible into the nearest one (by the windmill door); then quickly switch to your dagger when the second one rushes you. Best bet: Fight while backpedaling and popping mushrooms.

 Tip If the going gets too tough against the Spriggan duo, consider quaffing your Potion of Shield for a defensive boost. But use it only as a last resort. You'll want that potion even more against the Henchman you'll meet shortly.

 Get ready for more combat.

- Open the windmill door. Yikes! Another crossbow-wielding Spriggan.

- Rush through the door at the Spriggan and eliminate the vile pest.

WINDMILL (INTERIOR)

Not much in here. Just a bale of hay and an ax stuck up high on the wall. Axes are really good for chopping things. Do you think an ax would be helpful against slavering hordes of monstrous creatures? The answer: Yes, Connor, it would. Plus, it has other uses.

- Push the bale of hay under the ax. To do so, you must push the bale from two directions—toward the door, and then toward the center of the room.

- Hop onto the hay bale.

- Take the ax from the wall.

- Hop back down.

- Arm yourself with the ax and be sure your Health rating is at 100 percent. You're about to fight a very, very tough enemy.

- Exit the windmill.

WINDMILL (EXTERIOR):
THE FIRST HENCHMAN

As you exit the windmill, a powerful Henchman demands your Mask fragment. If you already used your Potion of Shield earlier, you'd better be at least a Level 5 Hero and loaded with health items to survive this ghastly encounter.

- Drink your Potion of Shield, if you have it.

- Kill the Henchman. (It's so easy to just *write* that, isn't it?)

Figure 1-11
The Ax Hop. Push the bale of hay under the ax in the windmill, and then jump atop the bale and snag thyself a most fearsome weapon.

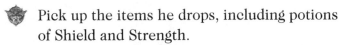

- Pick up the items he drops, including potions of Shield and Strength.

- Retrace your steps north and east over the bridge.

- Head south past the fountain.

- Take the first right to the mill.

Figure 1-12
The Henchman.
You don't know
what combat is
until you've tangled
with one of these
guys. Our advice:
Use a Potion of
Shield to survive.

THE MILL

🛡️ Don't miss the pair of mushrooms growing near the evergreen
tree to the right of the mill doorway.

🛡️ Enter the mill to trigger Connor's automatic observation, "I

Figure 1-13 Rope-and-Hook. You can't retrieve that handy climbing tool on the balcony wall until you stop the rolling grindstone, driven by the mill wheel outside.

could use that rope-and-hook." Unfortunately, the spinning grindstone blocks the way.

- Exit the mill and turn left.

- Walk around the side of the mill to the tall tree.

- Use your ax to chop down the tree.

The tree falls, stopping the flow of water to the wheel in back of the mill. The mill wheel stops turning, which in turn stops the grindstone inside. Now you can get up to that rope-and-hook.

- Go back inside the mill.

- Hop up onto the milling area.

- Hop up onto the balcony.

**Figure 1-14
Dam the
Environment.** Didn't
take long for that ax to
come in handy, did it?
Chop down the tree to
dam the flow to the
mill wheel.

- Take the rope-and-hook. As Connor says, it will prove useful for climbing.

- Exit the mill, head north, and then cross the bridge again.

- Go to the Kavanagh house.

KAVANAGH HOUSE

- Enter the Kavanagh house. (Mr. Kavanagh stands petrified just outside his gate.)

- Note the hobbyhorse and the child's drawings on the table. "A child must live here."

- Grab the mushrooms from the basket on the shelf.

- Exit the house.

KAVANAGH'S OUTHOUSE

- Go to the outhouse in the yard behind the Kavanagh house.
- Arm yourself with the ax, and then open the door. Surprise!
- After combat, continue northeast to the fence.
- Hop over the fence and proceed north along the river bank.

Figure 1-15
Head Rush. Wait! You didn't give him a chance to wipe!

THE WATERFALL

- Follow the river north toward the falls.
- As you approach the falls, click on the falling water.

Figure 1-16
Secret Passage. Hey.
Something's behind
those falls.

Connor notices something behind the falling water. Unfortunately, the force of the water is too great to pass through. How can you reduce the flow?

- Approach the stone wall on the left (west) side of the falls.

- Note the appearance of a "rope-and-hook arrow" at the lower right corner of your screen. This indicates that you can climb the waterfall.

- Click on the rope-and-hook in inventory.

- Click the rope-and-hook on the wall. Connor tosses the hook up and gets ready to climb.

- Go forward to climb to the top.

Figure 1-17
Fun with Grapnels.
Use your new rope-
and-hook to climb the
falls.

TOP OF FALLS

- Push the stone blocks off the table. This cuts off half of the stream's flow, revealing a tunnel behind the waterfall.

- Click your rope-and-hook on the wall to climb back down.

- Enter the tunnel.

As you step into the tunnel, *King's Quest: Mask of Eternity* asks if you want to load a new region, the Castle Daventry. And that answer would be, *Yes, Roberta, I do.*

Figure 1-18
Half a Fall. Push the stone blocks to dam half the stream. Now you can enter the secret tunnel.

TUNNEL BEHIND FALLS

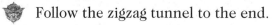 Follow the zigzag tunnel to the end.

Click on the candle (actually a hidden switch) to open the secret door.

Enter the castle's dining hall.

CASTLE DAVENTRY: DINING HALL

- Click on the wall portrait of the man: It's King Graham. Connor thinks it looks slightly off-center.

- Walk up against King Graham's portrait to push it, revealing a secret niche.

- Take the hefty brass key from the niche.

- Walk through the door at left.

- Pick up the torch ashes from the ground beneath the burned-out torch on the wall.

- Continue down the hallway into the throne room.

Figure 1-19
Key Discovery. Push the portrait of King Graham to open a hidden niche.

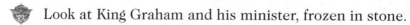

THRONE ROOM

Look at King Graham and his minister, frozen in stone.

Click on the mirror when it swirls.

An evil presence swirls into view, laughing at your puny efforts to foil his evil master play. Worse, he calls you a "stripling." Can you imagine a more humiliating insult? Before you can insult him back, he disappears.

Go back to the dining hall.

Exit the castle through the tunnel.

What now? This is a classic adventure game. In classic adventure games—when in doubt, explore.

Figure 1-20
The Bad Guy. Well, he didn't introduce himself. But his demeanor suggests foul corruption, don't you think?

TO THE OLD CASTLE RUINS

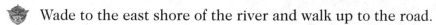

- Wade to the east shore of the river and walk up to the road.
- Follow the road north to the Daventry sign; then turn right and go east.
- Zombies! Five of them, in fact, rise up in your path. Kill them and gather dropped goodies.
- Continue east along the road.

Soon you see a stone mausoleum ahead, guarded by another tough Spriggan with a crossbow. Apparently, these guys always draw tomb duty. You could try to pick him off with your own crossbow from a cowardly distance, but, darn it, you're a hero. Start acting like one.

TOMB OF SIR JAMES

- Walk up to the near (south) wall of the tomb.
- Arm yourself with your ax.
- Hugging the wall, slip up to the wall's end. Then sprint around to the stairs, rush up, and gore the good fellow.

The Spriggan's bloody death releases the spirit of a dead hero, Sir James of Daventry, famous knight of yore. He says, "Hark, fellow Champion! Seek ye the Dimension of Death? Find the door of divine origin; the urn will reveal the way." You can click on Sir James to have him repeat his message. In fact, he'll repeat it again and again, forever, if for some perverse reason you choose to make him do so.

Figure 1-21
Sir James the Transparent. James was once a great hero. Now he's an incorporeal substance. Take his ring, but try not to join him just yet.

So now you have direction. Your first objective: Find the Dimension of Death. Fun!

- Whack open the tomb door with your ax.

- Enter the tomb and put away your ax.

- Push the lid off the sarcophagus. (Remember, you can't push objects while armed with a weapon.)

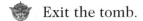 Take the hero's ring.

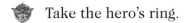 Exit the tomb.

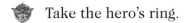 Cross the bridge over the moat, but stop before entering the castle keep ruins.

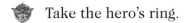 Wield your ax and prepare for battle.

CASTLE KEEP RUINS

Two more Spriggan guards wait in ambush just beyond the entry passage of the castlekeep, one on either side. This is a tough fight, so be sure you have plenty of healing items handy before you wade in.

 Defeat the pair of guards and plunder their mangy carcasses.

Figure 1-22
Castle Keep Ruins.
What nasty things lurk
therein? Follow your
ax through the gate.

- Keep your ax wielded!

- Climb up the nearby ramp. Another Spriggan is posted at the top, just around the corner to the left. Behead him most joyously.

- One more Spriggan guard lurks on this level. Find and kill him.

- With ax at the ready, climb up the last ramp to the lookout post.

The final Spriggan guard there is tough, but loaded. He drops a rugged leather breastplate and a bottle of Sacred Water. Now that he's exterminated the vermin, Connor can explore the lower keep fully.

- Click on the leather breastplate to wear it.

- Pick up the bottle of Sacred Water.

- Go down both ramps to ground level.

Figure 1-23
Leather Breastplate. The extra protection's nice. But the look is what counts, man.

CASTLE KEEP: TELEPORTER ROOM

- On the ground floor, enter the two side rooms and pull the three chain handles (two in one room, one in the other). This disarms a set of nearby booby traps.

- Enter the back hallway.

- Follow the hallway to the first corner. See that slot in the wall? It's one of the booby traps you disarmed by pulling the chain handles in the side rooms.

- Continue down the passage toward the locked doors.

You *did* pull the chain handles in the two side rooms on the ground floor, didn't you? If not, stepping into the patch of sunlight on the floor triggers three traps that shoot arrows from the far ends of the hall—two on one side, one on the other.

- Use the key (from the niche in King Graham's portrait) on the door to unlock it. The doors open automatically.

- Walk through the doorway.

This is the teleporter room. To teleport, stand on the magical pad and open your map. Scroll through the map to another world, where you've already found another teleporter, and then click the teleporter button beneath the map.

Of course, if you're following this walkthrough, this teleporter is the first magical pad you've found. So you can't go anywhere just yet. But it comes in quite handy later.

- Run out of the room and down the hall to the right, hugging the right-hand wall. You trigger the arrow traps, but if you hurry, you'll round the corner safely before getting hit from behind.

Figure 1-24
Teleporter. This swirling vortex works with your magic map to teleport you from region to region.

 Exit the ruined castlekeep.

 Head due east through a narrow pass in the hills. You encounter a huge beast sitting forlorn at a foul pond.

THE UNICORN/BEAST

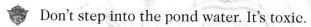 Don't step into the pond water. It's toxic.

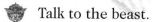 Talk to the beast.

You learn the pathetic creature is, in fact, a unicorn. But, as she tells you, a swamp witch took advantage of the evil tempest that descended on Daventry, and stole her horn. This witch, who the good beast says is not from Daventry, also poisoned the waters of the pond.

Keep clicking on the beast until she has nothing new to say. Being the kind of guy you are, you promise to help her, if possible.

Head south to the alchemist's house—the one with the boarded-up front door.

Figure 1-25
Hornless. This poor beast says it's a unicorn. *Yeah, right.*

ALCHEMIST'S HOUSE

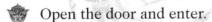 Bash out the boards over the door with your ax.

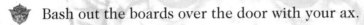 Open the door and enter.

Figure 1-26
Alchemist's House. Alchemists always have neat stuff. Break, enter, and take it all.

- Get the scroll for the Permanent Spell of Might.

- In your inventory, right-click on the scroll to see the ingredients you need: "A morsel of giant golden mushroom, a blue adamant, the tongue of a basilisk. Combine these under the blast of a lightning bolt." No problem!

- Get the Elixir of Life from the worktable.

- Get the Potion of Shield from the worktable.

- Go back to the church. Remember, it's down in the far south part of the map.

CHURCH (EXTERIOR)

- Approach the blocked front door. Aha! Your rope-and-hook arrow appears.

- Use your rope-and-hook on the wall.

- Climb to the roof.

- Approach the hole in the roof.

- Use your rope-and-hook on the hole.

- Climb down to the church floor.

CHURCH (INTERIOR)

- Take the candle burning on the side table in the entryway. (Connor calls it "a sacred flame.")

- Approach the large urn at the back of the church, near the lectern.

Aha! Remember the words of the spirit of Sir James: "Find the door of divine origin; the urn will reveal the way." Could this be the urn?

Figure 1-27
Church Breaking.
Hey, let's loot the
church! Grab
anything not nailed
down, and then go
push that urn by
the lectern.

Push the large urn. Through the window, you see the mausoleum door open.

Go back to the entryway.

Use your rope-and-hook on the wall and climb back up to the roof.

Figure 1-28
Open Tomb. When
you push the
church urn, the
mausoleum door
opens. Watch it
through the
window.

CHURCH ROOF

- On the roof, go to the opening in the wall.
- Use the rope-and-hook on the wall.
- Climb back down to the ground.

MAUSOLEUM

- Go around the church.
- Sprint through the graveyard into the now-open mausoleum. (Or stroll casually, if you feel like slaughtering some Zombies to build experience.)
- Step into the swirling light.

Figure 1-29
Shadow Bane. No weapon you own can hurt this monster. Looks like you need magic.

This triggers an encounter with a seemingly indestructible Shadow Bane who guards the entrance to the Dimension of Death. How can Connor defeat this dark, incorporeal beast? Who might know its secrets?

- Exit the mausoleum. Once again, the raven summons you.

- Sprint through the graveyard to avoid Zombies.

- Return to the half-frozen Wizard by the lake.

THE WIZARD

Click on the Wizard to trigger a conversation. He says only a magical illumination spell can defeat the Shadow Bane at the gate to the Dimension of Death. The Wizard can concoct such a spell, but he needs three things—a flame from a sacred place, a ring of a dead hero, and the ashes of a torch. Do you have any of those things?

- Give the "sacred flame" (the candle from the church) to the Wizard.

- Give the ring (from the sarcophagus of Sir James) to the Wizard.

- Give the torch ashes to the Wizard.

The Wizard quickly whips up a magical Ring of Illumination for you. But wait! You're not quite ready to go back to the mausoleum yet. You need one other item to make surviving the Dimension of Death *much* easier.

Figure 1-30
Light Ring. Give torch ashes, the hero's ring, and the church candle to the Wizard. He conjures up a useful little spell, plus you get a nice buzz out of the deal.

 Plunge into the lake behind the Wizard.

 Swim due west to the towering island in the middle of the lake.

WIZARD'S ISLAND

See the house atop the island's pinnacle of rock? That's the Wizard's home. Inside, you'll find some interesting things. But how do we get up there?

 Walk around the island to the "odd structure."

 Approach the rock wall directly behind the structure. The rope-and-hook arrow appears.

 Use your rope-and-hook on the wall and climb up.

 Open the door and enter the house.

Figure 1-31
House of Wizard.
Sure, it *looks*
inaccessible. But these
real estate developers
never take into
account a guy with a
rope-and-hook.

WIZARD'S HOUSE

- Take the Potion of Invisibility under the desk.

- Click on the magical quill in the ink bottle by the spell book. It writes a new parchment, inscribed with the symbol of the planet Jupiter.

- Take the parchment from the book.

- Use the parchment on the spinning celestial globe by the door.

- When the globe opens, take the Potion of Reveal inside.

- Turn toward the writing stand and drink the Potion of Reveal. An illusory chest appears near the writing stand.

Figure 1-32.
Hocus Pocus. Wizards always have weird stuff, such as magic quills that write magic pages that open celestial globes holding Potions of Reveal that reveal illusory chests holding great big silver bells.

 Open the illusory chest and take the large silver bell inside.

 Exit the house.

WIZARD'S ISLAND

- Use the rope-and-hook to climb back down the cliff.

- Step over to the "odd structure." Guess what? It's a bell stand.

- Use the silver bell on the bell stand.

- Wield your ax and strike the bell three times.

The Lady of the Lake appears, bearing a slick-looking weapon—the Sword of the Lake, a mighty weapon, indeed. Take it. You'll need it. Now you're ready to face the Dimension of Death.

- Click on the Lady of the Lake to get the sword.

- Swim back east across the lake.

- Return to the mausoleum by the church.

Figure 1-33
Fish Call. Whack the bell three times with your hand weapon to summon a special visitor from the lake.

Figure 1-34
Lady of the Lake.
She's got a really great
sword.

THE CHURCH MAUSOLEUM

Step into the vortex. The magical Ring of Illumination automatically
dispels the Shadow Bane.

CHAPTER 2

The Dimension of Death

as your *Mask of Eternity* manual points out, the Dimension of Death is "the holding place of souls awaiting judgment." It's also the hangout of a lot of nasty Skeletons who seem pretty bitter about that coat of flesh you're wearing over your bones. They want your soul, too. Most Skeletons are greedy that way.

1. Start (Portal to Daventry)
2. Altar of Azriel
3. Gate to Tile Puzzle
4. Fallen Warrior
5. Gate to Compound
6. Switch (to 7)
7. Arrow Traps
8. Switch (to 9)
9. Fireball Traps
10. Sylph Fountain Area
11. Southwest Tower
12. Trapped Child
13. Boathouse
14. Weeper/Pedestal
15. Fireball Traps
16. Switch (to 15)
17. Path to East Tower
18. East Tower
19. Square Key
20. Training Area
21. Dying Man
22. Central Tower
23. Hall of Respite
24. Hall of War
25. Hall of Immortality
26. Hall of Justice

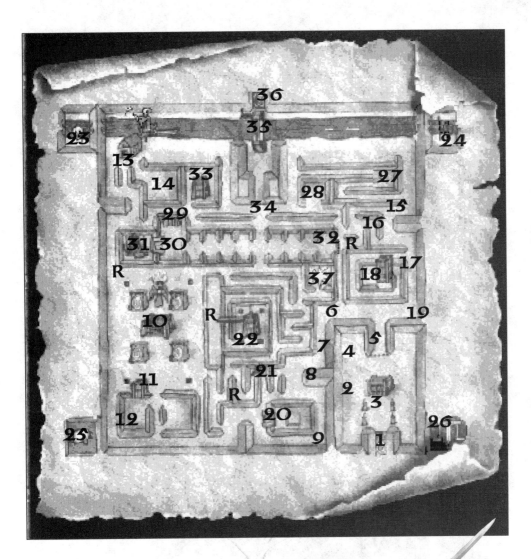

27. Blood Pool (Mold)
28. Many Urns!
29. Door to Jail
30. Illusory Door
31. Azriel's Hammer
32. Lever (to 34)

33. Northwest Tower (Potion of Reveal)
34. Gate
35. Bridge of Life
36. Portal to Swamp
R Rock

ENTRY HALL

First things first. Before you go anywhere, turn around and examine the five symbols above the portal vortex. For your convenience, here they are:

Figure 2-1
High Five. Here are the symbols above the portal to the Dimension of Death. You'll need them later.

Turn back around, draw your Sword of the Lake, and step forward into the darkness. This triggers an automatic encounter with a small squad of Skeleton guards.

Shatter the Skeletons and loot their remains.

Figure 2-2
Welcome to Hell. Now get the hell out.

Skeletons carry good stuff—health items, coins, and so on. But don't pick up any of their broadswords. They're weaker than your Sword of the Lake. If you accidentally snag a broadsword, just click on the Sword of the Lake on the ground and swap it back.

ALTAR OF AZRIEL (LEVER OF LIFE)

Walk northwest from where you first encountered the Skeletons. Look for a spinning object suspended over an altar before a horned stone idol.

Read the inscription on the altar: "E'er the Lever of Life spins 'round the Pedestals of Death to unlock the sacred Sanctum of Azriel, Lord of Death."

Take the spinning object, the Lever of Life.

Figure 2-3
Altar of Lord Azriel.
Pluck that spinning
Lever of Life out of
the air.

This lever activates all four of the Pedestals of Death—the four small pillars with burning flames—located nearby in the center of this cavernous entry hall. When all four pedestals are activated, the huge doors to the Main Hall open automatically.

THE FOUR PEDESTALS OF DEATH

The four Pedestals of Death the Lever of Life activates rise near the spot where you encountered the first Skeleton guards; two pedestals sit on either side of the stone pathway from the portal. Again, a flame burns atop each pedestal.

To use the Lever of Life on each pedestal:

 Insert the Lever of Life into the pedestal slot. (Just click the lever on the pedestal.)

Figure 2-4
Pedestal Pusher. Four of these pillars festoon the entry hall. Insert the Lever of Life into the triangular slot in each one; then "push" (walk up against) the lever to turn it.

- Put away any weapon you may carry.

- Walk Connor into the Lever of Life. He pushes it, rotating the pedestal and putting out the flame. Then he retrieves the lever automatically.

- When you rotate the fourth pedestal, huge doors nearby open in a most cool fashion. Zounds!

- Walk through the now-open doors.

FLOATING TILE PUZZLE

Remember the five symbols over the portal vortex? Those very symbols (and quite a few others) are etched on these floating tiles. Your task: *Jump from tile to tile in the exact order of the symbols (from left to right) etched over the portal.* Did you jot down the portal symbols? You could go back to the portal and do so now. But then, what kind of third-rate strategy guide would make you do such a thing? Read on.

Figure 2-5
Floating Tiles. They'd look nice in your bathroom, but of course you'd disintegrate every time you stepped out of your shower.

Before you start hopping tiles, note the following:

1. To jump onto the tile in front of you, simply press your forward movement button.
2. The target tile—that is, the tile you'll hop on when you press your forward movement button—is highlighted.

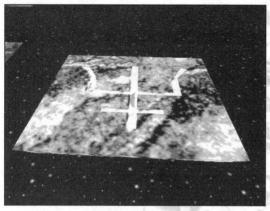

1. Turn right and hop down to the far end of the start platform, and then turn left and hop onto this tile with the first symbol.

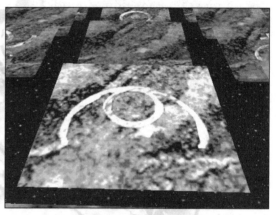

2. Hop down onto this tile with the second symbol.

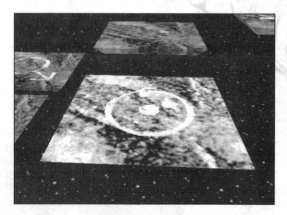

3. Hop onto this tile with the third symbol.

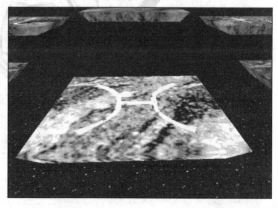

4. Hop onto this tile with the fourth symbol.

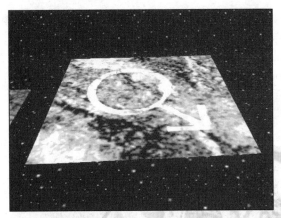

5. Hop onto this tile with the fifth
symbol.

LORD AZRIEL

Meet Azriel, Lord of the Dimension of Death. Believe it or not, he's on
your side. Not a bad guy, really. He seems a little skeptical of your
appointment as Champion Eternal, but he gives you a key to unlock
the gate to the Compound of Death. Azriel asserts you will find the

Figure 2-6
Hi, Lord of Death.
His guards have
revolted, and much
of his head is
missing. But Azriel
is on your side.

River of Death on the its far side. Apparently, you must cross this river to continue your journey to the Realm of the Sun, the sacred realm of the Mask of Eternity.

You end up back where you started, at the front of the entry hall.

THE FALLEN WARRIOR

Head over to the northwest corner of this hall, past Lord Azriel's altar.

Find the ring of boxes surrounding the fallen warrior. (When you read "fallen," think "dead.")

Break a box to reach the fallen warrior.

Click on the warrior to examine him. A piece of his shield falls off.

Take the piece of his broken iron shield.

Figure 2-7
Good Source of Iron.
This poor warrior holds a crumbling iron shield. Take a piece.

If you want, you can smash the surrounding boxes. One contains mushrooms, but others contain nasty Skeleton guards you can kill for an Experience rating boost.

GATE TO THE COMPOUND OF DEATH

Explore the rest of the entry hall. A few item-laden Skeleton guards roam the east end.

Go to the gate at the hall's north end. Careful! Two Skeleton guards are posted on the other side. (Try picking them off with your crossbow.)

Use Azriel's key on the gate.

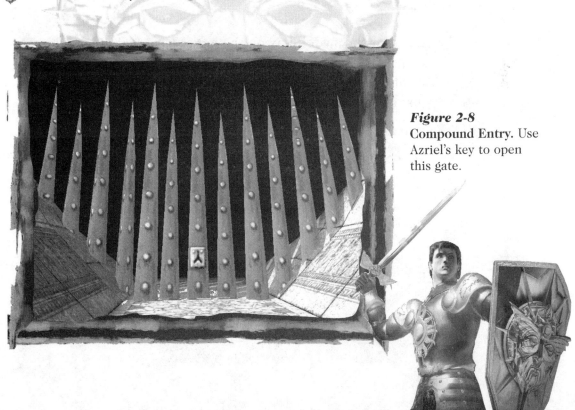

Figure 2-8
Compound Entry. Use Azriel's key to open this gate.

COMPOUND OF DEATH

 If you haven't already, defeat the first pair of Skeleton guards. A third shoots arrows from a distance. Go chop him into bone shards.

 Don't go east! It's almost certain death, at this point. Instead, go west.

> ## Tip
> Smash boxes and urns wherever you go in the Compound of Death. It's fun, and occasionally you find a health item or two. But break them from a distance with your crossbow, just in case a Skeleton or Wandering Spirit pops out.

 Look for the switch box on the left (south) wall. (See 6 on the map.) Be sure the switch is flipped down. This disarms a row of eight traps—little red-eyed skulls on the wall that spit arrows—just around the corner.

 Stick to the left wall as it curves around the next corner.

 Shoot the urns on the platform. (See 8 on the map.)

 Hop onto the platform, gather the health items, and flip down the wall switch. This disarms fire traps at the end of the hall to the south.

 Continue following the left wall, working to the southwest corner of the compound.

Figure 2-9
Trap Switch. Wall box switches throughout the compound usually control deadly arrow or fireball traps somewhere nearby.

At the southwest corner of the compound, you run into a bunch of Zombies and hear a young child crying. This is disturbing, but don't worry, we'll be back to help the child soon. For now, slay the Zombies and keep following the left wall as it angles north.

SYLPH OF INNER BEAUTY

After a few paces north, the compound opens into a large area full of odd, shrine-like structures with a water fountain in the middle. (See 10 on the map.) Big metal boxes sit at each of the four corners of this open area.

- Pick up any rocks you find.

- Drink from the fountain to restore your health. Take as many sips as you need. The healing is never-ending.

- Read all the inscriptions you can find. A pedestal on the outside corner of each structure reads, "Whoever, just and pure, lights the Torches of Righteousness, will meet the Sylph of Inner Beauty." Hey, let's give it a shot.

- Push the metal box in each of the four corners of this fountain area until the pressure plate pops up beneath it.

Figure 2-10
Magic Water. This fountain sits in the middle of an area of shrine-like structures. Drink from it to restore your health.

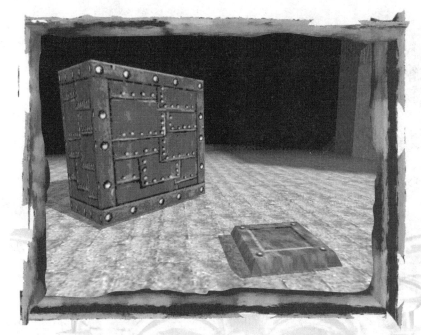

Figure 2-11
Pressure Plate. Push the four metal boxes in the corners of the open fountain area to release four pressure plates.

Don't miss the rock near the northwest metal box! You'll need rocks later.

When you push each box off its pressure plate, a torch lights atop a nearby pedestal. Yes, you just lighted the Torches of Righteousness. Go to the fountain to meet the Sylph of Inner Beauty. And yes, she's a babe.

Click on the Sylph to trigger a conversation. She warns you of the corrosive nature of the River of Death.

Click on the Sylph again. She says that with a little rust and mold, she can whip up a protective spell for you.

Go south to the passage just left of the tower structure. (You must look up to see the tower.)

Figure 2-12
But What about a
Boyfriend? The Sylph
needs mold and rust.

SOUTHWEST TOWER AND BOX ROOMS

A tall structure—let's call it the Southwest Tower—and two rooms full of boxes dominate this southwest corner. One room is easily accessible, but a large metal box blocks the other.

Box Room 1 (Pedestal)

- Enter the room to the left.

- Nail the two Skeleton guards, and then break boxes to get various health items.

- Read the inscription on the pedestal: "Three holds the key to Creation and the infinite multitude of beings and numbers." My, that's interesting.

- Exit the room.

Box Room 2 (Trapped Girl)

You have two ways to get into the room the metal box blocks: One, you can make a running jump over the box. Two, you can use your rope-and-hook to climb the outside wall of the tower, and then climb down inside the room.

In the room, break more boxes and gather items, including some healing Sacred Water.

Wait. Do you hear crying? Break through boxes to the young lass in the southwest corner of the room.

Listen to her woeful tale. Can you help her?

Of course you can. You're a hero. Go push the metal box as far away from the entry as possible. This triggers the girl's escape.

Exit the room and head northwest, past the Sylph's fountain area.

Figure 2-13
Lost Lass. The metal box in the doorway traps the poor child in this room. Be a good fellow and move it for her, will you?

RIVER OF DEATH

- Stick to the west wall. Three Skeleton archers block your path. Drill the poor bonehead bastards.

- Continue north along the left wall until you reach the riverbank. This is the River of Death.

- *Don't step in the water!*

- Dip the piece of iron shield (from the fallen warrior) into the river. The corrosive waters rust the iron. Aha! Now you need some mold.

- Enter the building just east of you.

BOAT DOCK

- Click on the spectral boatman to talk with him. When you ask for a lift across the river, he points out that his boat is incorporeal and you are not, and suggests you seek the Bridge of Life.

- Click again. When you mention foul pools of blood all about, he explains, "The Sacred Heart is wounded." Then he mentions something about a Deliverer.

- Click again. When you offer to be the Deliverer, he suggests you Attain Perfect Balance against the Feather of Truth on the Scales of Justice. You bet!

- Click again. The boatman tells you that to find the Feather of Truth you must seek the Hall of Respite. Then (and I quote), "Judge the skulls on the left. Down Creation. The one Complete stands out. Down Creation plus Completion equals All Things."

Figure 2-14
The Boatman. He can't offer you river passage, but he has some good information. Note in particular his cryptic advice about the Hall of Respite.

Exit the boathouse and veer slightly left into the open area with the pedestal and a Weeper.

PEDESTAL AND WEEPER

Pick off the Weeper with a crossbow bolt from a good distance. (If you get too close, Weepers suck the life right out of you.)

Read the pedestal: "Seven holds the key to the rhythms of life. The number of Completeness." Didn't the river boatman say something about Completion?

Exit the room and proceed east along the riverbank.

Figure 2-15
Grim Weeper. Weepers drain your Health, but they go down easy. Hit this guy from a distance. Then pick up a big clue from the pedestal inscription.

EXPLORING THE RIVER OF DEATH

I strongly suggest you explore the area, building up your Experience rating while gathering all-important rocks. (I'm serious; you'll need some rocks later.) And it's combat time. A lot of monsters want a piece of you now. Remember, the best defense is a good offense.

> **note** As you explore, keep a sharp eye out for rocks! You must gather four.

- Draw your sword and move east along the riverbank.

- Kill all monsters. In particular, watch for rising Zombies.

- Soon a wall blocks your eastward route. Turn south. Careful! A unit of three Skeletons lurks just around the corner.

- Stick to the left wall—you pass a spiky gate—until you get back to the river. Watch out for Skeleton archers posted high on walls. Take them out with your crossbow.

- At the river, turn right and head east again. Again, beware rising Zombies.

- At the wall (northeast corner of the compound), you must turn south.

- Head south, sticking to the left wall.

When you turn the next corner, watch for three fireball traps on the right (north) wall. Their control switch lies straight ahead and around the corner. (See 15 and 16 on the map.) But you can just turn south and stick to the left wall. The fireballs will miss you.

- Continue south until you get about one-third of the way down the map.

> **caution**
>
> Careful! If you go too far (about halfway down the map) you run into a very tough squad of five Skeleton goons. My advice: Avoid them for now.

- Look for a narrow path branching right. (See 17 on the map.)

- Follow the path as it circles upward to a tall tower emblazoned with glyphs of Lord Azriel. This is the East Tower.

EAST TOWER
(COMMANDER SKELETON)

- At the top of the path, walk to the tower wall until the rope-and-hook arrow appears.

- Use your rope-and-hook on the wall.

- *Save your game here!* You're about to face a powerful, heavily armored Commander Skeleton.

- Climb the wall.

Figure 2-16
The East Tower.
Climb up to the fight
of your life.

Figure 2-17
Tough Bones. Drive the tough East Tower guard over the edge. You'll take considerable damage in the process, so use a Potion of Shield, if you have one.

 If you have a Potion of Shield, now's a darn good time to use it. You can't kill this guy. Instead, you have to drive him back until he falls off the tower.

 A good tactic: Rather than drive the Commander Skeleton clear across the roof (and take a lot of damage in the process), wait for him at the tower's edge. When he advances to attack, run around behind him. Now you have him pinned near the edge.

Figure 2-18
Light Chain Mail. Be sure to pick up the Commander Skeleton's dropped armor.

After the Commander Skeleton falls, use your rope-and-hook to climb back down.

Take the path back down.

On the way, be sure to pick up the Commander Skeleton's Light Chain Mail.

By now you've probably built your Experience rating up to Level 12 or so. Add that new Light Chain Mail, and you're ready for some tougher challenges.

THE SQUARE KEY

When you reach the bottom of the East Tower path, turn right and go south.

Figure 2-19
The Square Key. This is
your reward for surviving
the vicious melee.

Five tough Skeletons guard both the corridor and a key box.
(See 19 on the map.) Pump them full of crossbow bolts, and
then finish them off with your sword.

Open the key box and take the square key.

Head west to the wall, and then south, working your way down
to the locked doors at 20 on the map.

SKELETON TRAINING ARENA

Use the square key on the doors. They open
and Connor automatically enters an arena with
a raised platform. Six frisky Skeletons fight and
wager. Fortunately, they're so caught up in
their activity they don't notice you.

Back up a few steps to the doorway.

Figure 2-20
Square Key Door. Use the square key to open these doors in the south compound area.

Figure 2-21
Another Key. Guys will be guys, whether they have flesh or not. Put a brutal end to their horseplay, and then pick up that circular key.

- Use your crossbow to shatter as many Skeletons as you can; then quickly switch to your sword for infighting.

- Loot the room. You find another golden key, this one circular.

- Exit, turn right, and go due north up the corridor with a patch of burning debris.

THE DYING MAN AND THE WEEPER

- Approach the wounded man sitting in the corner.

- Click on him. With his dying breath he tells you he's searching for the Hammer of Azriel, without which you can't cross the River of Death.

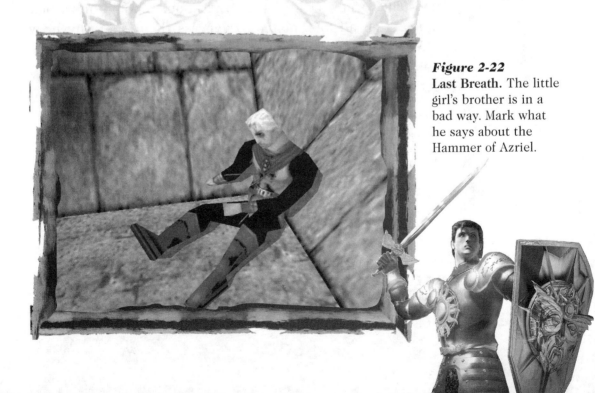

Figure 2-22
Last Breath. The little girl's brother is in a bad way. Mark what he says about the Hammer of Azriel.

- Continue around the corner. Don't miss the rock on the ground!

- Beware the Weeper waiting around the next corner. Hit him from afar, if you can.

- Continue north and east from the Weeper, down the passage with the fallen columns. You'll meet a Skeleton who drops a Potion of Strength when he crumbles, and a pair of archer Skeletons farther north.

- Follow the passage around to the Central Tower area. (See 22 on the map.)

CENTRAL TOWER: THE PORTAL PLATES

The Central Tower is surrounded by four pressure plates that activate very important portals back by the Sylph's fountain. You must place heavy objects on all four plates to depress them. Got any heavy objects? What about rocks? Of course, you probably have fewer than four rocks at this point. But another lies nearby.

To get another rock:

- Walk around the tower walls until you can use the rope-and-hook.

- Climb the tower.

- At the tower's top, walk west across the overpass.

note Read the engraved pedestal at the top of the Central Tower. It speaks of four Halls of Light. The four pressure plates on the ground below open portals to these hallowed halls.

◆ At the far side of the bridge, find the rock just north of the ramp.

◆ Now cross back to the tower.

◆ Use the rope-and-hook to climb back down.

◆ Place rocks on all four pressure plates.

If you're still short a rock or two, you could explore and find more, or peek at this chapter's map to see rock locations (each marked by an 'R'). However, there's an even quicker solution.

◆ Lure a Zombie over any pressure plate still unpressed.

◆ Kill the Zombie. He falls, depressing the plate. What a nice ghoul.

◆ When all four pressure plates are depressed, exit the Central Tower area and turn left.

◆ Zigzag up to the Teleporter Room. (See 37 on the map.)

Figure 2-23
The Easy Way. Toss rocks onto the pressure plates to depress them.

Figure 2-24
The Hard Way. See? Zombies are good for something. Lure one over a pressure plate and kill it to depress the plate.

TELEPORTER ROOM

Here's the teleporter for the Dimension of Death. This offers quick passage to any other region of the game where you've discovered similar teleports—Daventry, the Swamp, the Underground Realm of the Gnomes, the Barren Region, the Frozen Reaches, and the Realm of the Sun. In this walkthrough, so far, we've found only the one in Daventry.

You needn't use this teleport now (or ever, if you follow this walkthrough strictly.) Work your way back west to the Sylph's fountain.

SYLPH'S FOUNTAIN AREA: FOUR PORTALS

Those four shrine-like structures surrounding the Sylph's fountain now glow with swirling vortices, portals to the hidden Halls of Light in the four corners of the compound.

- Approach the northwest portal—the one with the inscription about "Eternal Respite."

- Arm yourself with the crossbow.

- Step through the swirling vortex.

Figure 2-25
Light Express. Portals like this one open near the Sylph's fountain when you depress the pressure plates at the Central Tower.

HALL OF RESPITE

This area is accessible only via the portal. If you press [Tab] to bring up your map, you'll see you've jumped to a secret hall off the northwest corner of the Compound of Death.

- Step forward and swivel left to shoot the Skeleton archers with your crossbow.

- Hop onto the lower block, and then to the taller block.

- Save your game!

- Be sure you're in Walk mode, and then walk *carefully* to the farthest edge of the taller block. You need every spare inch to make the following jump.

- Put away your crossbow and switch to Run mode.

- Make a running jump across the river. (It's not easy.)

- Get the Potion of Shield from the angel statue.

Look at that skull collection. They all look alike, don't they? You need the right one, though. Remember what the boatman at the River of Death said?

First, "Judge the skulls on the left." That would be the left cabinet of skulls here.

Second, "Down Creation." Remember the pedestal in the Box Room that reads, *Three holds the key to Creation*? Translate "Down Creation" to "Down three." Down three what? Down three shelves, of course. That would be the bottom shelf.

Third, "The one Complete stands out." Remember the pedestal in the room across from the boathouse that reads, *Seven holds the key to the rhythms of life. The number of Completeness*? The "one Complete" on the bottom shelf would be the seventh skull.

- From the left cabinet, bottom shelf, take the seventh skull from the left.

Figure 2-26
How to Get a Head. Just take it. But take the correct one—left cabinet, third shelf, seventh from the left.

Figure 2-27
Pushover. Find the cracked column. Then put your shoulder to it. After it falls, use it as a launching pad for your leap back across the river.

- Find the column with the crack and push it into the water.

- Use the fallen column to make a running jump back across the river.

- Exit the Hall of Respite through the portal.

SYLPH'S FOUNTAIN AREA

- Approach the northeast portal—the one with the inscription about war.

- Arm yourself with the crossbow.

- Step through the swirling vortex.

HALL OF WAR

- Step forward to the pedestal, swivel right, and shoot the Skeleton archer across the water.

- Move around the pedestal and shoot the Skeleton archer on this side of the river.

- Cross the bridge by walking carefully on the railing to the gap in the middle, hopping across the gap to the platform, and then walking carefully down the railing on the other side.

- Get the Potion of Strength from the anvil.

- Put the skull (from the Hall of Respite) on the headless statue.

The headless statue transforms into a noble warrior, and the Feather of Truth pops out of a niche onto the ground. Excellent! Now let's find the Scales of Justice and Attain Perfect Balance. Then we can Order Pizza and Watch Hours of Televised Sports.

- Pick up the Feather of Truth.

- Go back across the bridge, using the same careful technique as your previous crossing.

- Exit the hall through the portal.

Figure 2-28
Feather of Truth.
Put the skull from
the Hall of Respite
on the headless
statue to reveal the
feather you seek.

SYLPH'S FOUNTAIN AREA

Go through the southwest portal—the one with the
inscription about healing.

HALL OF IMMORTALITY

There it is—the Sacred Heart. The boatman said it's wounded. As you slog through the bloody slime of this hall, you'd have to concur.

- Pick up the Potion of Reveal.

- Exit through the portal.

Figure 2-29
Cardiology 101. I'm not a surgeon, but if a heart's not beating, my guess is that's a bad thing.

SYLPH'S FOUNTAIN AREA

Go through the southeast portal—the one with the inscription about Truth and Perfect Balance.

HALL OF JUSTICE

Lo! You've found the Scales of Justice. And not much else. This odd void actually appears on your map just outside the southeast corner of the Compound of Death. Remember how the boatman said you must "Attain Perfect Balance against the Feather of Truth"?

- Take the Potion of Invisibility hovering above the pedestal flame.

- Place the Feather of Truth on the scale.

- Step forward to hop onto the other side of the scale.

Hark! Is that a heartbeat? You bet your epaulets it is. The Sacred Heart is healed. And suddenly Lord Azriel appears, free, and grateful for your Champion Eternal deeds.

- Step forward to hop off the scale.

- Step forward again to exit through the portal.

Figure 2-30
What a Featherweight. Put the feather on the scales and hop aboard.

For fun, you can go back through the southwest portal and see the Sacred Heart beating happily. More good news: All the foul, toxic blood pools have dried up throughout the Compound of Death. And that means you now have access to a substance you've been seeking for the Sylph.

GETTING THE MOLD

- From the Sylph's fountain area, head north and work your way along the outside passages to the northeast corner of the compound.

- Just south of the river, go down a narrow passage that leads west. (See 27 on the map to find your destination.)

- As you turn the first corner in the passage, Connor says, "Phew! What's that moldy smell?" Aha!

Figure 2-31
Mold Spot. Once the Sacred Heart beats again, this blood pool drains, revealing the mold you seek for the Sylph.

- Continue to the now-drained blood pool.

- Pick up lots of mushrooms and, more importantly, the glob of green mold.

- Now return to the Sylph at her fountain area.

SYLPH'S FOUNTAIN

- Give the rusty iron shield piece to the Sylph.

- Give the green mold to the Sylph. She conjures a spell of protection and bestows it upon you, boosting your Armor rating by a few points. (Believe me—where you're going, you'll need it.)

- Exit the fountain area to the northwest and follow the north passage again.

- Follow the north passage around the right turn.

Figure 2-32
What an Angel. Give the mold and rusty piece of iron to the Sylph. She whips up a protection spell.

Go straight down the narrow passage east. (See 29 on the map for your destination.) Watch out for the Weeper! Nail him with crossbow bolts before he can get close.

JAIL SWITCH ROOM

Find the double doors on the south wall. (See 29 on the map.)

Use the circular gold key (from the Skeleton Training Arena) to open the doors.

Arm yourself and enter the jail.

A deadly Skeleton archer mans each of the six boxes in the entry area. Mow them all down with the weapon of your choice. You find yourself in a room full of wall switches. Large double doors lead west, and a massive barred gate leads east.

We'll get to the doors in a moment. First, let's check out the switches. The switches on these walls open the many gates and cells in the jail area. In general, you want to open all gates and cells. But I suggest you do so in the following manner.

East Wall Switches

The four switches on the east wall control the main gates in the jail area. This allows access to four blocks of jail cells; each cell block comprises four cells.

Flip down all four switches on the east wall.

The first switch opens the gate at the near (west) end of the two western blocks of jail cells.

The second switch opens the gate at the far (east) end of the two western blocks of jail cells.

Figure 2-33
Jail Switches. Wall switches control all the gates and cell doors in the jail area. Open everything.

The third switch opens the gate at the near (west) end of the two eastern blocks of jail cells.

The fourth switch opens the gate at the far (east) side of the two eastern blocks of jail cells.

Believe me, it sounds more complicated than it really is. Again, just throw all these east wall switches. Then go east through the now-open gates.

Use your crossbow to wipe out Skeleton guards and the Weeper prisoners behind bars in the all four cell blocks. If you keep your distance, it's a real turkey shoot, and prevents much damage later.

Go back west to the switch room.

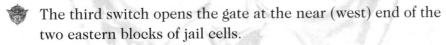
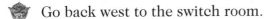

Figure 2-34
Losers Weepers.
Before you open the jail cells, wipe out the Weepers with your crossbow. Keep your distance, though. They can still suck you dry, even through the bars.

West Wall Switches

The four switches on the west wall direct power to each of the four blocks of jail cells. You can pull only one switch at a time. Each west switch directs power to a particular block of cells; then the four cells in that block can be opened using the four south wall switches.

South Wall Switches

The four switches on the south wall open each of the four individual jail cells in the particular cell block activated by the currently thrown west wall switch. Again, this all sounds horribly complicated, but basically, you want to open all jail cells, so just take the following steps.

- The first west wall switch is already down. Pull all four south wall switches to open the four jail cells in the northwest block.

- Pull the second west wall switch.

- Pull all four south wall switches to open the four jail cells in the northeast block.

Pull the third west wall switch.

Pull all four south wall switches to open the four jail cells in the southwest block.

Pull the fourth west wall switch.

Pull all four south wall switches to open the four jail cells in the southeast block.

See how simple it is? You just opened all 16 jail cells. Now it's time to wander merrily through the cells, gathering gold and other goodies. Be sure to break all urns to get Healing Crystals and other items.

In the last cell of the northeast block, pull the lever. This opens the main northern exit from the compound. Before we head there, we must acquire a very important item.

Arm yourself with the crossbow.

Return west to the switch room.

Figure 2-35
The Big Switch.
Pull this lever in
the last cell to open
the north gate to
the Bridge of Life.

HAMMER OF AZRIEL

- Turn to face the west double doors and use the Potion of Reveal. You see the doors are illusory.

- If you get closer, you also can see a big Egyptian-looking Skeleton warrior waiting on the other side.

- A good trick: Fire your crossbow through the illusory door at the Skeleton. You actually can kill him *before* you go through the doorway.

Figure 2-36
Revelation. The Potion of Reveal shows an illusory door with a big bad guy on the other side. Save yourself a headache and pepper him with crossbow bolts before you go through. Or go sword to sword, just for the fun of it.

Walk through the illusory door.

SHRINE OF AZRIEL'S HAMMER

A hammer spins on a floating altar in a shrine. That must be Azriel's hammer, the one mentioned by the little girl's dying brother. He said you need it to cross the River of Death. Guess what? He's right. But two very, very deadly Wandering Spirits patrol the altar. And as you should know by now, weapons can't harm these beings.

 Watch the Wandering Spirits. Notice that they patrol in a pattern.

 Approach the platform steps.

 Important: *Save your game here!*

 Make a careful "walking jump" onto the front edge of the main platform. (See Fig. 2-42.) Don't over-jump and get in the spirits' path!

 Switch to Run mode.

 Time your run and leap past the spirits onto the shrine platform. This may take many tries.

 Important: When you finally survive the leap, your Health rating is totally depleted. *Drink only Sacred Water to heal!* Mushrooms and crystals won't cut it here.

 Grab Azriel's hammer. Thankfully, the Wandering Spirits disappear.

 Go back through the illusory door into the Jail Switch Room.

 Exit the Jail Switch Room to the north, go right, and then take the first left and follow the path around to the northwest Tower (see 33 on the map).

Figure 2-37
Hammer of Azriel.
Those Wandering
Spirits are passive
killers, but killers
nonetheless. Hop
carefully to the
position shown
here, and then
make a running
jump to the altar.

NORTHWEST TOWER

The Northwest Tower features a two-level climb with your rope-and-hook. At the top you find four Healing Crystals and, more importantly, a Potion of Reveal (helpful in your eventual visit to the Frozen Reaches).

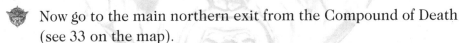 Now go to the main northern exit from the Compound of Death (see 33 on the map).

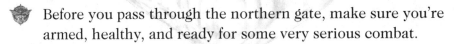 Before you pass through the northern gate, make sure you're armed, healthy, and ready for some very serious combat.

Tip You can save time in later regions by going back now to the Central Tower area (see 22 on the map) and picking up the rocks you put on the pressure plates. Rocks are quite useful in *Mask of Eternity* but are sometimes hard to find.

BRIDGE OF LIFE

When you pass through the now-open gate, a Commander Skeleton taunts you a bit, and then unleashes a six-unit squadron at you.

After you defeat the squadron, you must defeat the Commander. Drink a Potion of Shield, if you have one; he's very tough.

When the Commander Skeleton dies, he leaves some good stuff behind, including another Potion of Shield to replace the one you used. Be sure to pick up his powerful double-edged sword.

Look across the river. On the left side of the bridge you see a mechanical lever.

Arm yourself with the Hammer of Azriel.

Throw the hammer at the lever. This trips the bridge mechanism, lowering the drawbridge.

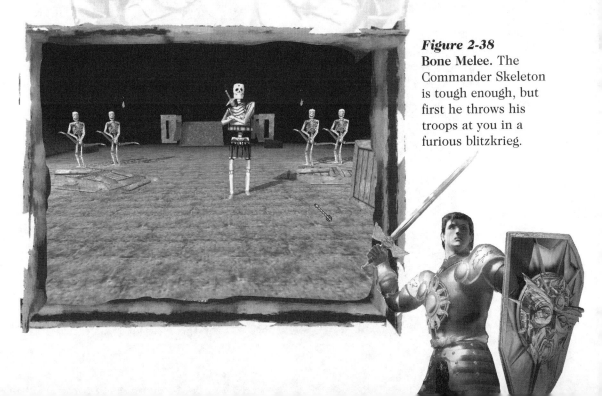

Figure 2-38
Bone Melee. The Commander Skeleton is tough enough, but first he throws his troops at you in a furious blitzkrieg.

Figure 2-39
Hammer Throw. See that mechanical lever just left of the drawbridge across the river? That lowers the bridge. Hit it with Azriel's hammer.

 Cross the bridge.

 Go through the portal on the other side to reach the Swamp.

CHAPTER 3
The Swamp

The Swamp is lovely, but probably not a good place to invest in real estate. The pea-green patches of water are toxic; plus, you'd have some pretty hostile neighbors. In fact, the idea of residential development drives swamp people to homicide. Keep your favorite weapon handy at all times.

caution

Beware swamp bubbles! They're the exhalations of an unseen, deadly creature. When you see or hear bubbles, throw your hammer or slash at the spot with your sword until you see a withering tentacle and black bubbles surface.

THE ORACLE OF THE TREE

From your starting point, work your way due west. Be sure to pluck the plentiful mushrooms on the way, and watch for Scavenger Slime, Swamp Fiends, and Bubble Monsters.

Find the thick-trunked tree up against the hill—the Oracle of the Tree. (See 2 on the map.)

Talk to the tree. It asks for gold in return for prophecy.

1. Start (Portal to
   Dimension of Death)
2. Oracle of the Tree
3. Swamp Shacks
4. Whispering Weeds
5. Golden Mushroom
6. Water Pump
7. Mandragor Grove
8. Many Carnivorous
   Plants!
9. Sprites
10. Swamp Witch Tower
11. West Tower
12. Teleporter

Figure 3-1
Root of Wisdom. Talk to the Oracle. He dispenses cryptic tips for one gold coin apiece.

Give gold to the tree. It says, "Where the Mask once sat, now doth sit a Pretender." You get a small jolt of Experience increase.

Keep giving gold until the tree has nothing more to say. You earn a few more boosts in your Experience rating.

Prophecies of the Tree Oracle

Here's a list of the tree's pronouncements:

"Deeds are fruits. Words are but leaves."

"Strength and righteousness grow stronger by being tried."

"Where the sinner cannot come, he shall send."

"He that doeth evil abhorreth the light."

"He who coveted all hath now brought on sin."

"Thou shalt go . . . thou shalt return. Never shalt thou perish."

"The Mask shall deliver victory unto the hand of the righteous."

"The Father of demons and abominations before the altar stands."

"He that would enter into a higher realm must have a good key."

"The Virtue of the Golden Ladle is within you. It shall purge the poison and restore the purity."

 From the Oracle of the Tree, head southwest.

 Find the pair of swamp shacks.

caution

Avoid the darker, pea-green areas of the Swamp. These are toxic areas. These areas are marked with skull and cross-bones on your magic map.

SWAMP SHACKS

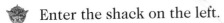 Enter the shack on the left.

Open the trunk in the corner and take the gold. (It's not considered theft when your victims are rocks.)

Swap your leather gloves for the metallic ones on the shelf in the other corner.

Figure 3-2
Swamp Shacks. Such a pleasant, rustic community. A relaxing place to break and enter.

- Exit and go to the other shack with the boarded-up door.

- Hack away the board with your weapon.

- Inside, open the chest and take the gold.

- Hack through the barricade on the inner doorway.

- Important: In the next room, pick up the Hearing Horn.

- Open the chest and take the gold.

- Exit the shack.

- Head northeast back toward the Oracle of the Tree; then veer southeast to the Whispering Weeds.

Figure 3-3
What? I said, *It's—
a—Hearing Horn!*

THE WHISPERING WEEDS

Hear that whispering? Something's going on. But if you get too close to the Whispering Weeds, they retract into the swamp. Fortunately, you have a Hearing Horn.

Figure 3-4
Whispering Weeds.
They know a really
good secret about the
witch. But you'll need
an amplification
device to hear it
clearly.

Get as close as possible to the Whispering Weeds without causing them to retract.

Use the Hearing Horn on the Whispering Weeds.

Aha! Did you hear that? "A Mask piece is in the Witch's Tower." This is formidable information, indeed. Go due north to the cove full of giant mushrooms.

MUSHROOM COVE

Wander about the cove plucking healthy mushrooms.

Work your way east to the back of the cove to find the Golden Mushroom.

Use your sword to hack off a piece of the Golden Mushroom.

Figure 3-5
Mushroom Cove.
These are all nice. But
you're looking for a
golden one.

Figure 3-6
Golden Mushroom.
Take that piece you
just hacked off.

 Take the piece. You now have one ingredient of the Permanent Spell of Might (as listed in the alchemist's scroll you picked up in Daventry).

 Continue north to the cove full of monstrous Mandragor Trees.

Tip Look for the water pump on the platform at the south edge of the Mandragor Grove. It's a refreshing way to boost your Health rating.

MANDRAGOR GROVE

 Work your way carefully around the outside of the cove, avoiding the dangerous roots of the Mandragor Trees.

Figure 3-7
Mandragor Trees.
Avoid these dangerous
fellows unless you
crave experience and
have a lot of health
items handy.

At the back (far north) end of the cove, find the skeleton with the bow.

 Tip

If you want to fight a Mandragor Tree, remember that you can't hurt it with a ranged weapon. Only your hand weapon works. Chop off both roots, and then quickly wade in close and slash at the trunk.

 Take the bow. (Yes, you're looting corpses.)

 Exit the Mandragor Cove.

Figure 3-8
Weapon Upgrade.
Swap Azriel's Hammer for this poor guy's sleek bow. I don't think he needs it anymore.

 Follow the curve of the hill to the right, toward the northwest corner of the map. Stay close to the hill to avoid poisonous waters.

TELEPORTER TOWER

On the way northwest, you'll see a tall scaffold-like wooden structure surrounded by poisonous waters. This region's teleporter device is located up at the top. Don't poison yourself trying to get to it just yet, though.

SWAMP WISPS

 As you wind north and west, hack your way through the dozens of Carnivorous Plants. (Or fire your new bow at them from a distance. It's great fun.)

Figure 3-9
Carnivorous Plants.
And you thought *your* lawn had problems. Do some weeding with your new bow and arrow.

- In the far northwest cove, talk to the Swamp Wisps. They ask for a secret in return for an antidote to the poisonous swamp waters.

- Click on the wisps again.

You tell them the secret you learned from the Whispering Weeds. In return, they unfold a flower before you. If you eat it, they say, you will no longer suffer from the poison of the swamp waters. They also insist you meet Mudge, the Swamp King.

- Click on the wisps again. They tell *you* a secret: Use the Golden Ladle on the waters to cleanse them of the poison.

- Take the flower. Connor eats it. Now you can travel through poisonous water without taking damage.

- Slog all the way down to the southeast corner of the map—the Swamp Witch's domain.

Figure 3-10
Wisp Swap. Trade the wisps a secret for this flower. Then eat it for total immunity to swamp poison.

Figure 3-11
Swamp Witch Tower.
Verily, what loathsome
practices transpire in
yon tower?

SWAMP WITCH'S TOWER
(EXTERIOR)

- Find the massive tower in the southeast corner of the map. (You can't miss it, really.)

- Save your game and get ready for a tough fight.

- Go around to the far (south) side of the tower. The Swamp Witch awaits. Warning: She's not a very pleasant person. Best bet: Quaff Potions of Strength and Shield, then attack with your sword.

- After you kill the witch, approach the grate-like door.

Figure 3-12
The Swamp Witch.
Two words—mutant
grub. And she's as
brutal as she is ugly.

- Look through the door. See the sandbags hanging by ropes on the back wall?

- Use your bow to shoot an arrow at the sandbag ropes. The door opens.

- Enter the tower.

SWAMP WITCH'S TOWER (FIRST FLOOR)

- Go into the room to the left and pick up the rocks in the corner.

- Go into the room to the right, the one with the dead Goblin on a slab.

Figure 3-13
That's Gotta Hurt.
Yank the unicorn horn from the chest of that pathetic Goblin corpse.

- Take the unicorn horn stuck in the Goblin's chest.

- Click on the cauldron. Watch the scene of Lucreto making his Henchmen.

- Click on the cauldron again. "So this is the source of yon poison!"

- Go to the foot of the ramp up, but don't climb yet.

- Click on the holes on the right-hand wall. Note also the blood-stains on the ramp. Suspicious, eh? They're arrow traps.

- As you climb the ramp, wave your sword in front of each hole to trip the arrow traps. (Each trap shoots only one arrow.)

WITCH'S TOWER
(SECOND FLOOR)

⬥ Explore the second floor. Break all the barrels to get an awesome assortment of health items.

⬥ Go outside onto the balcony and grab all the health items.

⬥ Go to the edge of the gruesome spike trap at the bottom of the ramp to the third floor.

⬥ Toss a rock onto the trap to spring it.

⬥ Go up the ramp to the third floor.

Figure 3-14
Spike Trap. Toss a rock on this bloody device to spring the trap.

WITCH'S TOWER
(THIRD FLOOR)

🛡️ Go up the east ramp and get the full suit of Chain Mail. Just in time, as you'll see.

🛡️ Get ready for tough combat. Go up the west ramp and open the chest to get the second piece of the Mask of Eternity. This triggers the appearance of one of Lucreto's Henchmen.

**Figure 3-15
How about a Hand?** Great, another Henchman. Quaff potions of Strength and Shield, and then whack off his foul hand. Don't forget to pick up your grisly prize.

- Kill the Henchman. In the process, you slice off his hand.

- Pick up the severed hand.

- Go back down the ramps and exit the tower.

- Cross the swamp to the northwest until you find a huge scaffold-like structure. (See 11 on the map.)

SWAMP BRIDGE AND GATE

- Climb the walled side of the structure with your rope-and-hook. You must climb two levels to reach the top.

- Cross the bridge to the gate.

- Note the hand-shaped keyhole on the gate. If you click on the keyhole, Connor tries to use his hand, but it's too small.

Figure 3-16
High Gate. Once you get the Henchman's hand, find this structure on the west side of the map.

Use the severed hand of the Henchman on the keyhole. The gate opens and Connor approaches a grid of stumps and stone pedestals.

STONE AND STUMP GRID PUZZLE

Only one correct path exists across this odd 6-by-7 grid. Step on any wrong stone or stump and an explosive charge detonates. To make matters worse, six pillars spit fireballs down the outside rows from the other side.

Here's some obvious advice: Save your game now and every time you make a correct move.

If you want to find the path yourself, toss rocks onto adjacent platforms to determine which is safe. You'll take a lot of fireball damage, though, so voraciously consume health items.

Figure 3-17
Stone-and-Stump
Grid

Or you can do it the old-fashioned way: Cheat. Here's the correct path:

When you make the final correct jump, you enter the Swamp Witch's secret vault automatically.

SECRET VAULT

Two powerful Swamp Fiends ambush you, one from either side. Kill them.

Open the chest and take the Golden Ladle.

Pull the two chain handles to open the switch box by the door.

Pull the switch in the switch box. This not only opens the gate, but also disarms the explosive charges in the grid.

Hop straight across to the other side. You walk out onto the bridge automatically.

Climb down the structure and return to the Witch's Tower.

WITCH'S TOWER

Go to the cauldron on the first floor.

Use the Golden Ladle on the cauldron.

This purifies all the poisonous waters in the swamp. It also triggers a sequence in which Connor meets Mudge, the King of the Swamp. Yes, he's a snail. As you might expect, he's most grateful. But there's no time to chat. Mudge quickly forms a whirlpool that leads to the Underground Realm of the Gnomes.

Now you have two choices: You can go on to the Gnome Realm or teleport back to Daventry to wrap up unfinished business. I suggest the latter, for no particular reason, other than that I know everything.

Figure 3-18
Better than Reverse Osmosis. Dip the Golden Ladle in the witch's vile cauldron to purify the swamp waters.

Figure 3-19
Meet Mudge. The grateful King of the Swamp opens a portal to the underground for you. But don't use it just yet.

BACK TO DAVENTRY

 Go up to the teleporter tower in the northwest part of the swamp.

Figure 3-20
Teleporter Tower. Climb this tower and take a quick trip back to Daventry to complete a side quest.

- Climb the tower with rope-and-hook.

- Stand on the teleporter swirl, scroll your magic map to Daventry, and then click on the teleport icon to make the jump to Daventry.

- Go to the beast/unicorn at the foul pool just east of the castle keep where you teleported in.

Figure 3-21
Good Deed Followup. Back in Daventry, give the unicorn her horn and check in on little Gwennie.

- Give the unicorn horn to the beast. She regains her true form and gives you a small crystal pyramid "dimmed by a mysterious darkness."

- Go to the Kavanagh house in the northwest part of Daventry. Gwennie, the young girl you rescued from the Dimension of Death, waits inside.

- Talk to Gwennie, take the gold she offers, and then talk to Gwennie again.

- Go back to the teleporter in the castle keep and teleport back to the Swamp.

RETURN TO THE SWAMP

Climb down the Teleporter Tower, return to the Witch's Tower, and step into the whirlpool to transport to the Underground Realm of the Gnomes.

CHAPTER 4

Underground Realm of the Gnomes

This realm of twisting subterranean passages was sealed off from the surface world by the same evil maelstrom that shattered the Mask of Eternity. The Gnomish mines are doubly infested: Rock Demons rise from the floors, and Bat Mantas drop from the ceilings. As you wander the tunnels you also meet the occasional Gnome. Some are friendly—usually because they're merchants with wares to sell. Others are busy burrowing with pickaxes and have no time to talk. They want out. Wouldn't you?

ENTRY HALL

- Scout this entry area for rocks and health items. Pluck mushrooms and break open all barrels.

- Arm yourself for combat. Your hand weapon will serve you best in these mines. A bow and arrow is ineffective against the many Rock Demons you encounter.

- Use a rock on the pressure plate to open the main door. Watch for the Bat Manta hovering on the other side.

- Enter the Realm.

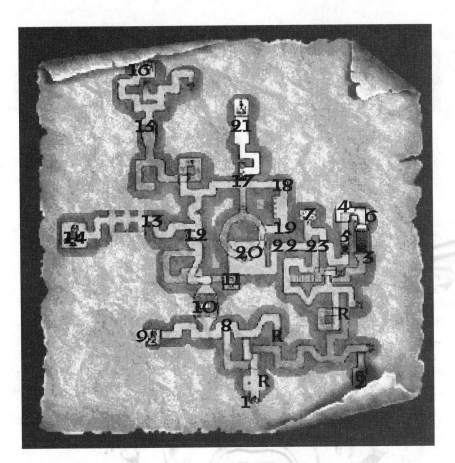

1. Start (Portal to Swamp)
2. Armor Shop
3. Zombie Swarm!
4. Old Man
5. Open Pit!
6. Amberglow
7. Teleporter
8. Top of Ramp
9. Weapon Shop
10. Turning Bridge
11. Apothecary
12. Padlocked Door
13. Rolling Boulder Trap
14. Sage Gnome
15. Wall Climb
16. Tree Root
17. Bricked-Up Wall
18. Two Rock Demons!
19. Wall Climb
20. Boulder/Hole
21. Dragon Wyrm
22. Wall Button (opens 23)
23. Hidden Passage
R   Rock

Figure 4-1
Door Jam. Put a rock on the pressure plate to hold the door open.

SOUTHEAST MINES

- From the main door, head east. A Rock Demon lurks just around the first corner.

- Break barrels and gather health items and rocks.

- When you reach the dead end, turn around and go back past the main door.

- Take the first left to descend a slope that angles back east under the entry hall.

- Continue zigzagging east to the dead end; then go through the door on your right, leading south. (See 2 on the map for your destination.)

GNOME ARMOR SHOP

The Gnome armor merchant is a jolly fellow, proud of his wares. And well he should be. Arrayed on the table before him are a Bronze Breastplate for 350 gold coins and a Plate Mail Breastplate for 250 gold coins. Of course, you already have a fine suit of Chain Mail, but upgrade if you can afford it.

 Buy the best armor you can afford. To purchase, don the suit you wish to buy, and then give coins to the merchant.

 Exit the Gnome Armor Shop.

Figure 4-2
Gnome Armor. Trade up if you can afford it. Bronze is best, but Plate Mail isn't shabby.

SOUTHEAST MINES

- Step out of the Gnome Armor Shop and go left.

- Go right (north) at the first fork.

- Follow the corridor to the ascending ramp.

- Kill the hopping Spriggan, and take care not to fall into the open shaft under the ramp.

- Go under the ramp to find a cornucopia of health items.

- Climb the ramp.

- At the top, go left (west), smash the Rock Demon, and continue west down the twisting corridor.

- Enter the first corridor that branches right. It leads down stone stairs, heading east.

Figure 4-3
Zombie Swarm! A few paces after you go down the stone steps in the eastern mines, this welcoming party rises to meet you.

- Warning! When you reach the far east passage and turn north, a gaggle of Zombies rises from the ground. Decimate them.

- Cross the narrow bridge and continue north to the old bearded fellow stoking a fire.

- Click on the old man.

THE OLD MAN AND THE CRYSTAL

This ancient fellow claims to be tending the tiny remaining spark of faith of the once-proud race that dwelt in these tunnels. He says, "Only the Enlightened One can ignite faith." Then he speaks of the Light of Life. When Connor asks where one might gain this Light of Life, the old man answers, "It is everywhere . . . and nowhere." Why can't anyone just say what they mean?

Figure 4-4
Light Motif. The old man has some interesting things to say about light. But the most important spark here is that crystal next to him.

- Use a weapon to whack off a shard from next to the old man.

- Pick up the Elixir of Life on the ground nearby.

- Retrace your path back over the narrow bridge and up the stone stairs. (Hop to get up some of the steeper stairs.)

- At the top of the stairs, go right.

- Follow the corridor and keep bearing right when you have a choice of directions. Eventually you reach an open pit blocking your progress.

THE AMBERGLOW

- Save your game here!

- Hop over the pit.

Figure 4-5
Amberglow. Knock off a chunk of this stuff and take it. It's an ingredient you'll need later.

🛡 Continue up the passage to a dead-end room guarded by a bevy of Bat Mantas.

🛡 See the gleaming gold stuff encrusting the wall? That's amberglow. Whack off a chunk with your sword.

🛡 Take the chunk of amberglow.

TELEPORTER ROOM

🛡 From the amberglow room, retrace your route past the pit. (Save before you hop!)

🛡 Take the first passage that branches to the right (north).

🛡 Follow this passage to the teleporter room.

This is just a brief mapping exercise. Don't use the teleporter yet. But you'll need to come back later. It's the only way to leave this level.

At this point it seems natural to keep working west into uncharted areas of the mines. But consider taking another route, one that will better prepare you for the adventures to come. It requires a little backtracking, but it's worth it.

🛡 Return to the main door area (working south, and then west), where you started the level.

🛡 When you reach the top of the ramp to the main door area (see 8 on the map), turn left and work your way west.

🛡 Continue past the opening with pressure plates on the floor on your right. (We'll visit here in a minute.)

🛡 Proceed west to the doors and enter the weapon shop. (See 9 on the map.)

GNOME WEAPON SHOP

The weaponer has a fine trio of weapons for sale. From left to right: a heavy compound crossbow for 300 gold coins, a small compound crossbow for 200 gold coins, and a fierce war hammer for 400 gold coins.

- Buy the best you can afford, leaving at least 250–300 gold coins in your purse. If you manage to walk out with both the heavy compound crossbow *and* the war hammer, woe betide thine enemies, dude.

- Exit and go back up the corridor.

- Take the first left turn.

Figure 4-6
Hail, Outlander!
Welcome to the
Gnome Weapon Shop.

Figure 4-7 Good Arms. How about a war hammer for crushing Rock Demons? Or a heavy compound crossbow for picking off those annoying Bat Mantas? Either is a significant upgrade from your current weapon. Buy both if you can afford them.

THE TURNING BRIDGE

Three pressure plates control the movements of a bridge suspended over a wide shaft. The plate on the left rotates the bridge so it spans the shaft. The other two plates lower the ramps on either side of the bridge, extending it fully across the shaft. If you don't have at least three rocks, you've got some rock-hunting to do. (For rock locations, see R on the map.) Otherwise:

 First, place a rock on the left pressure plate. This rotates the bridge. (You must do this step first. The bridge can't rotate if either ramp is down.)

Figure 4-8
First Rock. Put a rock on the leftmost pressure plate first. If you lower either ramp first, the bridge can't rotate.

- Place rocks on the other two pressure plates to lower the bridge ramps.

- Cross the bridge.

- Follow the passage and take the first left. This leads down, around, and under.

Figure 4-9
Want Some of This, Slate Boy? Your new war hammer shatters rock most expeditiously.

APOTHECARY

The purveyor of healing items and magical potions sells the Potion of Shield for 75 gold coins, the Potion of Invisibility for 100 gold coins, the Potion of Strength for 50 gold coins, curative mushrooms for 3 gold coins apiece, and Healing Crystals for 20 gold coins apiece.

- Click on the statue to the right. The apothecary tells you it's Essence of Sun Tsu, a powerful strength enhancer. She says she needs three items before she can sell it to you—an object of iron, some tree root, and a bit of amberglow.

- Stock up on any other items you desire, but leave at least 250 gold coins in your purse. (You need this much to purchase the Essence of Sun Tsu later.)

- Exit the shop and climb the ramp.

Figure 4-10
Apothecary. This fine Gnome woman sells curatives and other good stuff.

Figure 4-11
Sun Tsu! Gesundheit.
Now turn your
attention to that
glorified chess piece in
the corner.

THE IRON LOCK

- At the top of the ramp, turn left and go to the padlocked doors.

- Whack off the iron lock with your hand weapon. (The war hammer works quite nicely.)

- Take the broken iron lock.

- Stay armed and ready! When you open the doors, a Spriggan waits on the other side.

- Kill the Spriggan and continue north.

- Take the first left and head west. Hear that rumbling?

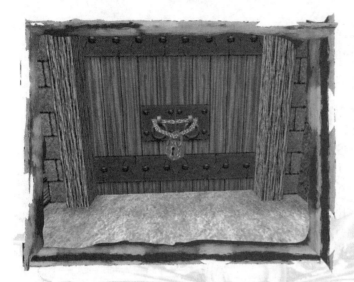

Figure 4-12
**Another Good
Source of Iron.**
Bash off that lock
and add it to your
inventory.

THE ROLLING BOULDERS

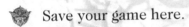 Save your game here.

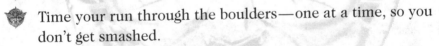 Time your run through the boulders—one at a time, so you
don't get smashed.

Figure 4-13
Rolling Rock.
Sprint past the
boulder traps in
Run mode.

 Watch out for the Rock Demon at the end of the hall!

 Continue through the door at the end of the passage.

THE SAGE GNOME

Approach the Sage Gnome and click on him to trigger a conversation. Connor admits he's lost in his search for the Mask pieces and tells of his magic map. The sage ponders the problem, and then offers to manipulate the teleporter system using his "terracosmic electromagnetic defibrillator" (the odd machine behind him). Unfortunately, the apparatus needs a new lodestone for magnetic power. Can you find one?

 Exit the room.

 Run back through the rolling boulders.

Figure 4-14
Sage Gnome. He can get you to the next region via teleporter. But first he needs a working lodestone.

THE UNDERGROUND CLIFF

- From the end of the rolling-boulder corridor, go left (north) up the main hallway.

- At the T intersection, go left (west) and proceed down the ramp.

- Continue along the passage and take the first right into a big empty room. (See 15 on the map.)

Looks like a dead end, doesn't it? But look up. The passage continues at the top of the cliff-like wall. Time to climb.

- Climb the wall with your rope-and-hook.

- Proceed to the T intersection; then go left and follow the passage into the big room. Beware of several pairs of Manta Bats on the way.

Figure 4-15
No Obstacle. This wall would look impassable to a guy without a rope-and-hook. Fortunately, you're not that guy.

TREE ROOT ROOM

Note all the tree roots twined over the walls and ceiling: This room must be fairly near the surface. Say, didn't the apothecary list "tree root" as one of her Essence of Sun Tsu ingredients?

- Hack off a piece of the tree root sticking out of the wall in the northwest corner of the room.

- Exit the room.

Figure 4-16
Root Room. Chop off a piece of that big tree root growing through the wall. It's one of the Sun Tsu ingredients.

BOULDER TRACK

- From the tree root room, go back to the cliff wall (at 15 on the map).

- Use your rope-and-hook to climb down.

Figure 4-17
Brick Wall. Why would anybody want to brick up a perfectly good passageway? Let's find out!

Go up the winding ramp and head east to the middle of the map. There, a bricked-up wall covers an opening. (See 17 on the map.)

Continue east up the slope. Two Rock Demons leer down from the top.

Figure 4-18
Rocky Road Ahead. Two angry Rock Demons are posted just up the slope from the bricked-up wall.

- Drink a Potion of Shield, if you have more than one, and destroy the Rock Demons.

- Proceed south to another wall. Climb it with your rope-and-hook.

- At the top, follow the passage into a large room with a boulder and a big hole in the floor.

- Push the boulder into the hole. It lands on a circular track below.

- Hop down into the hole.

- Push the boulder around the circular corridor. When you reach the ramp, Connor shoves it down automatically. The boulder smashes through the bricked-up passage at the bottom.

Figure 4-19
Anybody for Monster Billiards? Round object, round hole. What an amazing coincidence.

Figure 4-20
Sisyphean Fun. Push the boulder around the circle track to the ramp. It rolls down and smashes through the bricked-up passage, revealing a new area.

 Follow the boulder's path through the shattered wall and enter the new area. Don't go far!

THE BLACK DRAGON WYRM

Say, why do you suppose they bricked up this passage? Maybe you don't want to know. By the way, it's very dark in this new area. Wouldn't some light be nice?

 Use the crystal shard (from the old man tending the fire) on the purplish wall receptacle near the boulder. This lights all wall lamps in the area.

Figure 4-21
Crystal Light. Put the old man's crystal in the purple wall receptacle near the boulder.

- Arm yourself with your hand weapon. The Dragon Wyrm's thick hide is impervious to ranged weapons.

- Proceed down the passage to the Dragon Wyrm's lair.

- *Save your game here!*

- Advice: Drink potions of both Shield and Strength.

- Kill the Dragon Wyrm. It shrivels, leaving behind its black diamond heart on the floor.

- Take the black diamond.

- Go into the next room.

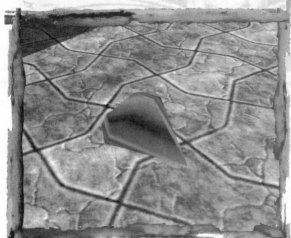

Figure 4-22
Have a Heart. After
you slay the Dragon
Wyrm, pick up its
black diamond
heart.

CRYSTAL ROOM

 Click on the purplish diamond "switch"
(right side of the crystal pedestal) and watch
the message. Someone who calls himself "the
prophet Hector" tells Connor about the Mask of
Eternity, betrayed by one of its own archons.

Figure 4-23
Crystal Clear.
Hector fills in some backstory and gives you another crystal pyramid.

- When Hector offers you a bright crystal pyramid, take it from the top of the pedestal.

- Put the darkened pyramid you got from the unicorn in Daventry on top of the crystal pedestal.

- Click on the diamond switch again to see another message. This one's from the bad guy. His message is to someone named Uriel, and it's not pleasant.

- Take back the dark crystal.

- Take the lodestone from the top of the pedestal.

- Go back to the Sage Gnome.

SAGE GNOME

- Give the lodestone to the sage. He puts it in his machine and opens a portal to the Barren Region. (Open your magic map and scroll it to see the Barren Region as a blank page.)

- Go back to the apothecary.

Figure 4-24
Lodestone Delivery.
The Sage Gnome's
machine tears this
universe a new
portal.

APOTHECARY

 Give her the three ingredients—the tree root, the iron lock, and the amberglow.

Figure 4-25
Get Sun Tsu-ed.
Give the apothecary
the three
ingredients she
seeks, plus a hefty
250 gold coin sum,
to get a dose of Sun
Tsu and a weapon
rating boost.

 If you have the 250 gold coins required, click your gold coin icon on the Sun Tsu statue to be imbued with the essence. Your hand weapon rating gets a boost.

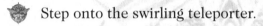 Now go back to the teleporter room.

TELEPORTER ROOM

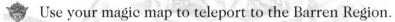 Step onto the swirling teleporter.

Use your magic map to teleport to the Barren Region.

CHAPTER 5

The Barren Region

Τhis godforsaken land is home to Fire Ants, Pyro Demons, and the dreaded Basilisk. A few hardy Weirdlings, Hill Men, and Fire Dwarves also manage to eke out an existence here. This is a very painful land to visit. In my experience, the Barren Region drained my health stores more than any previous region.

START: ANT HILLS

When you arrive, you see red Fire Ants scurrying around, doing what Fire Ants do. What is that, exactly? Gathering magma, is my guess. In

Figure 5-1
Orkin Nightmare. They're big, they bite, and they don't like you. If you get too close to a wandering Fire Ant, expect a sudden ant swarm.

146

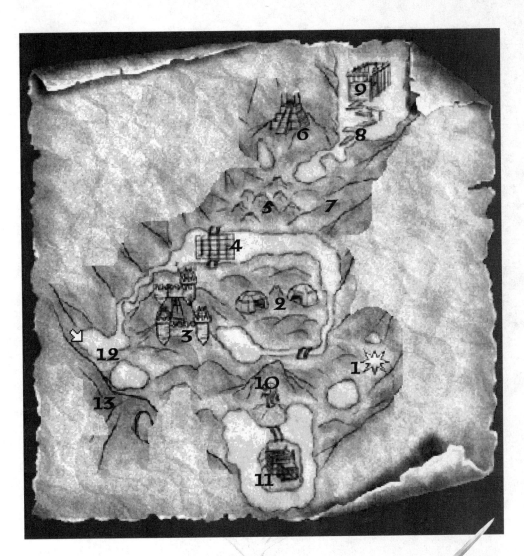

1. Start (Portal to Gnome Realm)
2. Weirdling Village
3. Sanctuary of the Stone of Order
4. Floating Blocks Puzzle
5. Lava Geysers
6. Pyramid (Fire Gem)
7. Mountain Pass
8. Stone Bridges
9. Gong Puzzle
10. Basilisk Lair
11. Temple
12. Narrow Crossing
13. Fire Dwarf Lair

Figure 5-2
Pyro Demon. I really hate these guys. You can't wade in after them, so pump them full of crossbow bolts until they burst into flames.

any case, they go about their business and pay no attention to your arrival, unless you get too close, or shoot one. If you catch just one ant's attention—well, expect a swarm, and expect to take a serious amount of damage.

🛡 From your arrival point, go west to the bridge. Watch out for Pyro Demons rising from the lava river!

🛡 Cross the bridge.

THE WEIRDLING VILLAGE

🛡 From the bridge, follow the path north to a pair of huts. This is a *very* small village of Weirdlings.

🛡 Enter the east hut.

Figure 5-3
Weirdling Village.
Let's go inside and see
if these folks live up to
their name.

WEIRDLING WEAPON SHOP

The Weirdling weaponer has a lovely battle-ax you can buy for 500 gold coins, but his ranged weapons are no better than the one you already have (if you purchased the heavy compound crossbow in the Gnome Weapon Shop). He speaks of the deadly Basilisk south of here, and says he knows how to make a weapon to kill it—a black diamond pike. He just needs a black diamond and a strong metal shaft.

Yes, you already *have* a black diamond—the heart of the Dragon Wyrm you slew in the Gnome Realm. So keep an eye peeled for a metal shaft.

 If you can afford the battle-ax, buy it.

 Exit and go to the west hut.

Figure 5-4
Weirdling Weaponer. His wares on display are mediocre, but he can make a nifty Basilisk slayer if you can provide the pieces.

WEIRDLING SHAMAN HUT

 Talk to the shaman woman. She claims she can heal the sick, cure the dying, banish evil spirits, and even resurrect the dead . . . for 25 gold coins, of course.

Figure 5-5
Shaman. She can cast healing spells for a small fee. Return to her if you get low on health items.

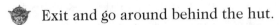 Exit and go around behind the hut.

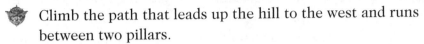 Climb the path that leads up the hill to the west and runs between two pillars.

SANCTUARY OF THE STONE OF ORDER

Climb into the fortress and cross the footbridge. The guards ignore you. Apparently, you're too puny to be considered a threat.

Talk to the creature with the really big horn.

Figure 5-6
Hey, Horatio. He's got a hell of a horn, but he wants the Stone of Order back on that altar.

This fellow, a Hill Man, tells you the Stone of Order disappeared during the vile storm, and nobody knows where it is. He says, "Only the rightful Upholder of Law and Order can seek the Stone." He adds that the Stone will reveal itself only to the true Upholder. His tone suggests this couldn't *possibly* be you.

🛡 Enter the Blacksmith Shop.

🛡 Talk to the blacksmith.

The blacksmith no doubt makes a strong shaft, but he doesn't do business with outlanders. That would be you. But suppose you did something really great for the Hill Men. Like, say, return their sacred Stone of Order. You might get a shaft out of the deal.

🛡 Exit the Sanctuary and go back down the hill.

🛡 Head northwest to the broken bridge.

Figure 5-7
Is That Good or Bad News? This guy won't give you the shaft.

BROKEN BRIDGE: THE "PRIME BOXES" PUZZLE

When you step onto the bridge, a grid of stone blocks surfaces in the river. These might form a nice hopping path to the other side if they didn't bob below the molten lava. But this is a puzzle, there's a solution, and you hold a strategy guide in your hands. So read on.

Seven of the blocks turn into metal boxes and stop bobbing when you jump on them. These metal boxes each have a symbol on top. The symbol represents a number; the total number of lines in the symbol is the number represented. For example, a line is 1, a triangle is 3, a box is 4, a box-and-triangle is 7, a five-pointed star is 10.

Your task: Jump across the bobbing blocks to these boxes in order of their numbers, from least to greatest—coincidentally, the first seven prime numbers—3, 5, 7, 11, 13, 17, 19. Needless to say, don't get caught on a block that sinks into the lava. It's gruesome.

Figure 5-8
Hot Blocks. Hop across in the right order, or die trying.

One other thing: When you jump atop the metal boxes in the correct order, each emits a sound—a number of percussive beats equal to the number of lines in the symbol on the box. So if you hear a drumbeat when you land on a box, you know you hit the right one in the order prescribed. Conversely, if you land on a metal box but *don't* hear a drumbeat, you've landed on a box in the wrong order.

The following diagram shows you which boxes are "prime" boxes:

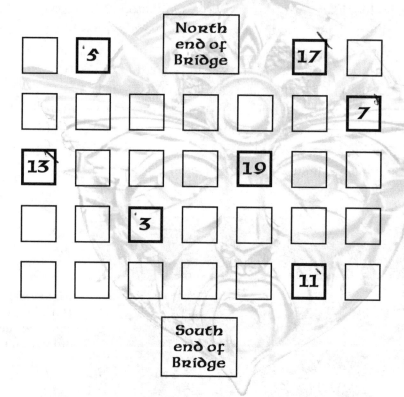

Tip

In general, try to jump onto the next box as it rises from the lava. This gives you the most time to align yourself and time your next jump. Another tip: Save your game each time you reach a "prime" box (one that turns to metal).

Starting from the bridge, jump these directions in the order listed:

1. Jump N, NW (Box 3)

2. Jump NW, N, N (Box 5)

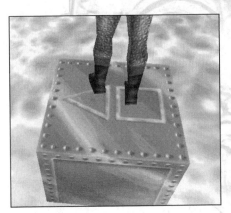

3. Jump SE, E, E, E, E (Box 7)

4. Jump SW, S, S (Box 11)

5. Jump W, W, W, NW, NW (Box 13)

6. Jump NE, E, E, E, NE (Box 17)

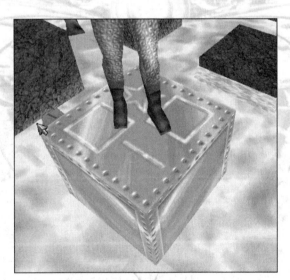

7. Jump S, SW (Box 19)

When you reach the final box in the correct order, metal boxes line up between the bridge ramps.

Hop across the metal boxes to the north bank.

Figure 5-9
Success! When you
jump on the boxes
in the correct order,
these five metal
boxes form a
permanent bridge.

LAVA GEYSER FIELD

Head north through the field of lava geysers. Don't get too close!
Geyser spray inflicts damage.

Continue climbing northwest past the geyser field to the stone
pyramid.

Figure 5-10
Avoid Molten Spit.
Keep your distance
from these geysers.

THE FIRE GEM

- Walk up the pyramid ramp to the top. A glowing fire gem sits on a stone altar.

- Take the fire gem. This releases a spirit—an archon, to be exact, a former acolyte of Lucreto, the evil incarnate who unleashed the storm and seeks the Mask.

- Go back south into the lava geyser field.

- Turn east and proceed through the mountain pass down to the river.

Figure 5-11
Plenty of Spirit. An archon hops from the fire gem with a warning about the Evil One. "He waits for thee, Connor of Daventry."

THE STONE BRIDGES

- Save your game here.
- Arm yourself with your ranged weapon. Several pairs of Pyro Demons lurk in this lava lake.
- Cross the disconnected series of stone bridge sections to the tall structure. Save your game after each successful jump.

Figure 5-12
Disconnected.
Whoever built this
bridge majored in
Cubist Engineering. Be
sure to save after you
leap to each new
section.

caution

Don't jump to the final three bridge sections leading east unless you want those health crystals on the last section. However, a veritable platoon of Pyro Demons attacks when you reach that end. Our advice: Forget the crystals.

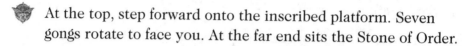When you reach the tall structure, climb it with your rope-and-hook.

At the top, step forward onto the inscribed platform. Seven gongs rotate to face you. At the far end sits the Stone of Order.

Pull out your ranged weapon and start shooting gongs.

Figure 5-13
Going, Going, Gong. Shoot the colored gongs in the order of the rainbow to complete the bridge to the Stone of Order.

Note that each gong has a color and pitch when you shoot it. You must shoot the gongs—you guessed it—in the correct order. That order happens to be the order of the rainbow, color-wise, and the order of the major scale, pitch-wise.

So the correct color order is red, orange, yellow, green, light blue, dark blue, and purple. Of course, you have to figure out which gong is which color. To do this, either shoot the gongs and take notes, or do the truly intelligent thing and simply read the next bullet point.

- Number the gongs from left to right and shoot them in the following order: 4, 2, 7, 5, 1, 3, 6.

- Each time you shoot a gong in its correct place in the order, another piece of the magical bridge forms under you.

- When the bridge is complete, take the Stone of Order.

- Take the stone back to the Sanctuary of the Stone of Order—the fortress on the hill above the Weirdling village.

SANCTUARY OF THE STONE OF ORDER

- Put the Stone of Order on the pedestal next to the guy with the really big horn. Suddenly, you're everyone's buddy.

- Go into the Blacksmith Shop.

- Click on the blacksmith. He gives you a strong metal shaft.

- Exit and go back down the hill to the Weirdling Weapon Shop.

WEIRDLING WEAPON SHOP

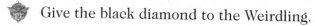 Give the black diamond to the Weirdling.

Give the metal shaft to the Weirdling.

Give gold coins to the Weirdling.

Figure 5-14
No Piker. Hey, the little guy knows what he's doing. In moments he crafts a killer pike from the black diamond and stout metal shaft you provided.

The little fellow accepts a mere 10 coins in payment. Then he crafts a magnificent black diamond pike for you. Is that a bargain, or what? Now all you have to do is stick it into a drooling gargantuan beast of unimaginable proportions.

- Exit the village and head south.

- Cross over the bridge and continue south to the Basilisk lair.

THE BASILISK LAIR

If you approach this monster face to face, pike or no pike, you're flame-broiled meat. Go ahead and try, if you want. Just be sure to save your game before you attempt anything so monumentally foolish.

- Head west up the slope that runs behind the Basilisk.

- Veer left (southeast) through the pass. It leads to a bunch of stone blocks in the lava.

Figure 5-15
Hero Time. There it is—the Basilisk. Now what? Try a rear approach by climbing the ridge behind it.

Jump across the blocks to the cliff on the other side.

caution

Careful! These block jumps look simple, but they can be tricky. As always, save after each successful jump.

Climb the cliff with your rope-and-hook. You find yourself above and behind the Basilisk.

Arm yourself with the black diamond pike (as if I needed to tell you that).

Step forward.

Figure 5-16
Rasslin' Basilisks.
Connor makes a most
impressive move on
the bloody reptile.

Connor makes a stunning leap onto the Basilisk's neck and rams home the pike. After the mutant worm dies, the pike won't come back out. Don't worry. You don't need it anymore. Believe me, that was the best 10 gold coins you ever spent.

TEMPLE (EXTERIOR)

- Arm yourself with a ranged weapon. Pyro Demons lurk.
- Cross the nearby bridge.
- Go around to the right side of the massive stone Temple.
- Climb the wall with your rope-and-hook.
- On top, approach the hole in the roof.
- Use your rope-and-hook to climb down the hole.

TEMPLE (INTERIOR)

- Click on the dead Fire Dwarf. He drops a granite key.
- Pick up the granite key.
- Click on the square wall panel to discover a hidden bottle of Sacred Water.

Look at the series of four symbols repeated on the wall. See the tiny arrows above and below them? Note the direction, which signifies an order to the symbols—crescent, triangle, circle, square. Note also that these four symbols appear on four pressure plates, one on each side of the sarcophagus in the middle of the room.

- Direct Connor to walk into the sarcophagus's four pressure plates in this order: crescent, triangle, circle, square. This opens a door.

Figure 5-17
Dwarf Key. Shake a
granite key loose from
that dead Fire Dwarf.

Figure 5-18
Wall Clue. The order of the symbols
on the wall signifies the order you
must push the plates on sarcophagus.

- Take the longsword off the sarcophagus. It's free!

- Go through the open door.

- Click on the square wall panel and get another hidden bottle of Sacred Water.

- Put on the full suit of armor. Heavy protection! This gives you a significant armor boost.

- Go back to the wall near the dead Dwarf.

- Climb back up using the rope-and-hook.

- From the roof, descend the outside wall and go back to the Basilisk.

Figure 5-19
Nice Reward. This full suit of armor in the hidden room boosts your Armor rating quite a few points.

BASILISK LAIR

- Use your new sword to slice off the Basilisk's tongue.

- Pick up the tongue. *Mmmm.*

- Now head back over the ridge behind the lair—the same one you crossed to get behind the Basilisk earlier.

- When you get to the fork, veer right this time.

- Work your way north, and then west, until you find a dead tree near a narrow strip of land between the lava lakes.

- Get your crossbow ready. A pair of Pyro Demons lurks nearby in the lava.

- Cross the narrow strip of land.

- On the other side, turn left and head south.

Figure 5-20
Give Me Some Tongue. Take a sword swipe at that dead Basilisk head. Then grab what drops.

Figure 5-21
Isthmus. This narrow crossing leads to the Fire Dwarf Lair. Keep your crossbow ready for the Pyro Demons in the lava lake.

FIRE DWARF LAIR (EXTERIOR)

- Continue south along the cliffs until you find two Fire Dwarves guarding the entrance to their underground lair.

- Kill the guards.

caution

If you back too close to the lava lake, another Pyro Demon may emerge behind you and complicate your battle with the Fire Dwarf guards.

Figure 5-22
Or Try the Salsa!
Meet the Fire Dwarf
Welcoming
Committee. They
really want you to
taste their Arrow
Flambé.

- Find the lock in the rock wall.

- Use the granite key (from the dead Fire Dwarf in the Temple) in the lock. The door opens.

- Enter the lair.

FIRE DWARF LAIR (INTERIOR)

- Follow the stone walkway, eliminating guards as you go. At its end you find three buttons on the north wall.

- Shoot the buttons to extend three ramps.

- Cross the first (leftmost) ramp.

JAIL CELLS (SNOW QUEEN)

- Turn the valve on the wall to release Freesa, the Snow Queen. She opens a secret door for you, and then leaves.

- Get the pipe cap on the floor in the leftmost cell.

- Arm yourself with your longsword. Get ready! A hammer-wielding Fire Dwarf guard is posted in the next room.

- Go through the now-open secret door and slay the Fire Dwarf guard.

- Examine the wall safe. Do those symbols look familiar?

Figure 5-23
She's a Snow Queen. And we mean that in a good way. She's grateful enough to open a secret door for you. Imagine how grateful she'll be if you can find her lost crystal scepter.

Figure 5-24
Safe Combo. Push crescent, triangle, circle, square to get yourself another really cool pipe cap.

Click on them in the same order you used on the Temple sarcophagus: crescent, triangle, circle, square. The safe opens to reveal . . . another pipe cap?

Exit this area and cross the second (middle) ramp.

STORE ROOM

Open the chest. This triggers another Henchman attack. Guess what? You found another piece of the Mask of Eternity.

Eliminate the Henchman.

Exit this room and cross the third (rightmost) ramp.

Figure 5-25 Mask of Eternity, Part 3. Oh, those pesky Henchmen! Looks like you can count on meeting one every time you grab a piece of the Mask.

STEAM ELEVATOR

- Careful! Another hammer-wielding Fire Dwarf waits in the back room. Cleave him.

- Put a pipe cap on one of the steam pipes. (Don't cap *both* steam pipes just yet!)

- Step onto the elevator platform.

- Use your ranged weapon to shoot the button on the far wall. The steam elevator takes you for a wild ride up one level.

- Step out and grab the crystal scepter and the Potion of Reveal.

- Get back on the elevator platform.

- Shoot the button on the far wall. Another wild ride—this time back down to the main level.

Figure 5-26
Going Up? After you cap one (and only one) steam pipe, hop onto the elevator and shoot the button on the far wall. Then hang on tight.

- Put the other pipe cap on the other steam pipe.

- Get back on the elevator platform.

- Shoot the button on the far wall. You blast off to the Frozen Reaches.

CHAPTER 6

The Frozen Reaches

amazing that these snowy reaches are but an elevator ride from the lava-scorched landscape of the Barren Region. A great icy lake splits the area map; you arrive on the south shore, near a stunning palace guarded by Snow Nymphs. All in all, not a bad place to start.

THE SNOW PALACE

Figure 6-1
Freesa Redux. Freesa is queen of the Snow Nymphs. She has a dragon you can borrow, but only if you return her lost scepter.

1. Start (Elevator to Barren Region)
2. Snow Palace
3. Dragon Pen
4. Dragon on Lakeshore
5. East Watchtower
6. Frost Demons
7. Invisible Snow Mane
8. Flame Sword
9. Narrow Pass
10. Frigid Lake
11. Guard House
12. Ice Lord Stronghold
13. Gryph Cave
14. West Watchtower
15. Northwest Pillar
16. Drake
17. Teleporter

🦁 Enter the palace.

🦁 Talk to Queen Freesa (the one with the crown).

Queen Freesa thanks you again for rescuing her from the sweltering Fire Dwarf lair, and gives you a quick overview of the situation in this frigid, snowy land. Her legions of Snow Nymphs are at odds with the Gryphs, a race of winged beings. Gryphs aren't normally hostile, but after their king was imprisoned in the castle of the Ice Lord across the great icy lake, relations between the Gryphs and Snow Nymphs grew, well, frosty.

If the Gryph King can be liberated, Freesa suggests, perhaps peace will result. Connor offers to help. The queen explains that the lake can be crossed only by air. She gives you permission to use her crystal dragon for transport, but first you must return her crystal scepter, which controls the beast.

🦁 Offer the crystal scepter to Queen Freesa. As she says, *you* need it more than she does.

🦁 Exit the snow palace.

🦁 Follow the icy path east to the crystal dragon pen.

CRYSTAL DRAGON PEN

🦁 Use the crystal scepter on the crystal dragon. She can't fly until the door is open, she explains. But the pull-chain lies broken on the floor.

🦁 Push the large ice block across the frozen pond until it's under the segment of chain hanging from the ceiling.

🦁 Make a running jump onto the ice block.

178

Tip The leap onto the ice block can be tricky. I had good success with a back-flip. Move a few paces from the ice block, turn your back to it, and then execute the back-flip by pushing your Back and Jump keys.

Pull the chain to open the pen gate.

Use the crystal scepter on the dragon again. Off you go!

Figure 6-2
Block and Chain.
Push the big ice block under the ceiling chain. Then hop atop the block and pull the chain.

Figure 6-3
Don't Look Down.
The crystal dragon flies you to the far shore of the great icy lake.

EAST WATCHTOWER

The dragon hauls you over the lake to the northern shore, where it deposits you safely and promises to wait for your return.

- After you arrive, proceed up the icy trail to the northwest.

- Veer left at the first fork.

- Veer right at the next fork and climb to the stone watchtower, where two Ice Orcs open fire with their deadly ice crossbows.

- After you kill them, swap your ranged weapon for one of the awesome ice crossbows they drop.

- The watchtower door is locked, so approach the tower wall and climb it with your rope-and-hook.

Figure 6-4
Hero Fodder. These unfriendly Ice Orcs must die to furnish you a weapon upgrade—a crossbow that fires bolts of ice.

- At the top, walk through the room to the opposite balcony.

- Pull the lever to open the trapdoor.

- Jump down through the open trapdoor.

- Inside, break the barrels to find numerous health items and potions.

- Open the chest and take the four Potions of Strength.

- Pull the nearby lever to open the main door.

- Exit and go north from the tower.

- At the crossroads, follow the path east. (Go to 6 on the map.)

FROST DEMONS/ INVISIBLE SNOW MANE

Up ahead, a very large pack of Frost Demons plods around in a dull rage. They hate you. Why? *Because you're walking on their ice!*

Frost Demons are slow, ponderous creatures. But they can take a lot of punishment, and here they have you greatly outnumbered. I found three ways to approach this confrontation. First alternative: Quaff potions of Shield and Strength, and then wade into the pack, slicing off hunks of Demon steak. Second alternative, for the potion-less: Wage a retreating, hit-and-run battle, backing down the path. I like the third alternative best; details follow.

- Run past the Frost Demon pack. (It's easy. They're slow.)

- Sprint northeast up the main trail.

- Near the top of the hill, you encounter a huge Snow Mane hunkering at the top of the path. One big problem: it's invisible.

Figure 6-5
The Frost Brigade.
Frost Demons run in packs. Advice: Don't fight them until you acquire the Flame Sword.

Figure 6-6
Snow Rat. The invisible Snow Mane is basically a big, tough rat with a hostile attitude. Start with a Potion of Reveal to locate the vermin; then drink other potions to beef up your combat rating.

- Immediately quaff a Potion of Reveal to see the beast.

- We also recommend you drink potions of Shield and Strength (if you have them).

- Kill quickly! The Frost Demon pack is still lumbering up the hill in pursuit. Don't let them sneak up from behind.

- After you kill the Snow Mane, sprint north to the frozen pond just ahead. The pursuing Frost Demons peel off and leave you alone.

Why this alternative? Because you're about to obtain a mighty hand weapon that puts your current sword to shame. This new weapon will make subsequent combat with the Frost Demon pack much, much easier.

THE FLAME SWORD

Step onto the frozen pond. Connor points out that the ice is thin. See that flaming sword encased in ice? Do you suppose a hot blade might be an effective weapon in a land where everything seems icy and frozen? Do you want that sword? How many stupid rhetorical questions can I ask in a row?

> ## note
> You need at least one rock to get the Flame Sword. If you don't have one, well, gee, that's kind of a drag. Travel back to the Dimension of Death or the Gnome Realm to get one. (See those maps for rock locations.)

- Toss a rock onto the ice. The ice cracks.

- Pick up the rock and toss it onto the ice again. The ice cracks more.

- Pick up the rock and toss it a third time. The rock shatters the ice and disappears into the pond.

- Use the fire gem (from the Barren Region) on the pond. The gem melts both the pond and the ice encasing the Flame Sword.

- Take the Flame Sword.

- Try to read the pillar. You can't decipher the markings . . . yet.

- If you avoided the Frost Demon pack earlier, go slay it now and rack up some serious Experience points.

- Work your way back down to the East Watchtower and continue south.

- Turn right (west) at the first fork and go through the narrow cut in the cliffs. (See 9 on the map.)

Figure 6-7
Cracking Up. Toss a rock three times onto the frozen pond. Then use the fire gem from the Barren Region to melt the shattered ice.

- Follow the path as it curves south through another narrow cut to another trail.

- Turn *hard* right and head north up the trail. (See 10 on the map for your destination.) Beware another lumbering Frost Demon pack!

FRIGID LAKE/GUARDHOUSE

At the top of the trail you come to a deadly cold mountain lake. On the far shore rises the citadel of the Ice Lord. Two of his Ice Orc minions stand guard at the front gate and open fire if you get too close. A guardhouse, currently empty, stands to your right. Let's make a supply run.

caution

Don't step in the water! Wading in the Frigid Lake means instant death, so don't skirt the lake to the west. You can't get around that side without stepping into the lake.

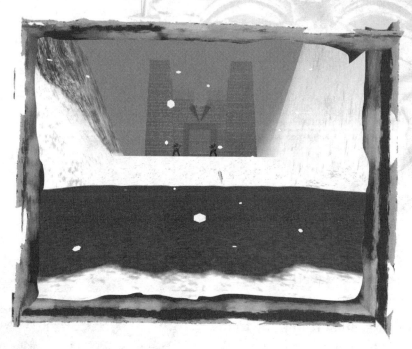

Figure 6-8
Frigid Lake. The Ice Lord's stronghold sits across some killer water. Go around the right (east) side of the lake and keep your feet dry.

- Enter the guardhouse.

- Break open the barrels and grab the goodies.

- Exit and move forward to the lakeshore. *Don't step in the water!*

- Pick off the pair of Ice Orc guards with your ice crossbow.

- Go around the right (east) side of the lake. Again, the water is deadly cold. Hug the cliffs as you go!

ICE LORD STRONGHOLD
(EXTERIOR)

- Go around to the rear (north side) of the stronghold.

- Climb the wall with your rope-and-hook.

- Walk to the grate on the rooftop. This triggers an automatic sequence in which Lucreto appears before the Ice Orc lord. What kind of parent names their kid Thork? No wonder he's such a thug.

- Go forward into the rooftop jail area.

- Talk to the imprisoned Gryph King.

- Pull the lever next to the ominous-looking chair across the room. Zounds! (Do you recall a certain spell that requires a lightning-bolt blast?)

- Walk to the small front balcony area. The scene switches to an overhead view.

- Step forward to trigger an automatic sequence. Connor leaps down and terminates the Ice Orc guard captain.

Figure 6-9
Free Bird. You need a key to spring the Gryph King. Try the Ice Orc guard below the front balcony.

Figure 6-10
Shocking Decor. That chair is perfect for a tongue-and-mushroom roast, but you still need a blue adamant.

Figure 6-11
Orc Ambush. This guy
thinks he's pretty
sneaky, but he's about
to take an ice shard
through the thorax.

- Pick up the jailer's key the guard captain dropped.

- Return to the rear (north side) of the stronghold and climb back
  to the roof with your rope-and-hook.

- Use the key on the cell lock to free the Gryph King.

- After he flies off, step out onto the roof. Another guard jumps
  Connor, and the two combatants fall through the grate into
  Thork's throne room.

THORK'S THRONE ROOM

- Defeat Thork. He's tough, so consider using
  potions of Shield and/or Strength.

Figure 6-12
Thork Nemesis. He's big, he's bad, and he's got the best name in the game.

- Get the deciphering amulet from the chest in the corner. Now you can read those Orcish pillars on the trails.

- Pick up the ice shard from the floor.

- Glance into the nearby barred room to see a frozen Henchman and a chest. You don't suppose it holds a Mask piece, do you?

- Look at the slot by the door. As Connor says, "Could be a locking device. Perhaps something fits there."

- Open the front door. Connor tries to walk out and nearly trips on the "wide gap" in the doorway. Hmmm.

Time for some real ingenuity. You need something to deactivate the locking device, something that goes in a slot. You have an ice shard. You have a suspiciously slot-shaped gap in the doorway. You have a Flame Sword. And by now, you should also have an ice crossbow with bolts that freeze anything they strike. Go ahead, take a few weeks to think about this. I'll be right here when you get back.

Figure 6-13
Simple Logic. It's
so obvious: just put
the ice shard in the
doorway gap, melt
it, freeze it, and
voila, you have a
homemade Orc-
unlocking device.

- Place the ice shard in the doorway gap.

- Use the Flame Sword on the ice shard to melt it. The water fills the doorway gap.

- Use the ice crossbow to re-freeze the water in the shape of the gap. You've just made an ice lever.

- Pick up the ice lever.

- Use the ice lever on the slot by the barred door. It works!

- Enter the room. Connor punches out the frozen Henchman and takes the fourth piece of the Mask from the chest. Unfortunately, the Henchman manages a complicated feat of reconstruction and attacks in the name of his master.

- Destroy the Henchman. Again, consider helpful potions to aid combat.

- Exit the stronghold and return south to the crystal dragon. Remember to round the east side of Frigid Lake! (It's on your left now.)

- Fly the dragon back across the lake.

GRYPH CAVE

- From the dragon's pen, proceed south and west past Queen Freesa's Snow Palace.

- Continue northwest up the trail to the Gryph Cave.

- Talk to the Gryph King. In thanks, he gives you a blue adamant.

- Go back to the dragon, fly north across the great lake, and return to the roof of the Ice Lord's stronghold.

Figure 6-14
Gryph Gratitude. He may think it a "mere bauble," but the King's blue adamant gift is just what you need for your Permanent Spell of Might.

ICE LORD'S STRONGHOLD
(ROOF JAIL AREA)

- Put the three ingredients of the Permanent Spell of Might—blue adamant, Basilisk tongue, and slice of golden mushroom—on the chair.

- Pull the lever to activate the chair's electrical bolt and conjure the spell. Check out the nice boost to your armor and weapon ratings.

caution

Climb down from the stronghold roof with rope-and-hook, the way you came up. Don't jump through the hole into the throne room! You won't survive the fall.

Figure 6-15
Spell of Might. Put the blue adamant, Basilisk tongue, and golden mushroom on the chair, and then give them a good jolt. They return the favor.

- Use your rope-and-hook to climb back down the back wall of the stronghold.

- Go through the cut in the hills on the west side of the stronghold.

- Eliminate the two Ice Orcs posted there.

- Follow the trail as it curves south. Two more pairs of Ice Orcs guard the path.

- Continue south until the West Watchtower appears to your right.

WEST WATCHTOWER

- Two more Ice Orcs guard the tower. Deprive them of their right to live.

- Go around the right side of the tower. A Frost Demon stands on the path below.

- Save yourself a bit of trouble later by sniping the Frost Demon with your ice crossbow.

- Don't bother climbing this watchtower; there's nothing on the roof.

- Enter the tower, break barrels, and scavenge the plentiful potions and crystals.

- Go back down to the main trail and follow it northwest to the pillar.

NORTHWEST PILLAR/ FROST DEMON PACK

- Use your deciphering amulet (from Thork's throne room) to read the inscription on the pillar: "Only a blade of fire can sever the heads of the drake."

- Continue northwest up the trail. Another swarm of Frost Demons descends on you. Gore the big furry goofs.

Figure 6-16
Northwest Pillar.
"Only a blade of fire
can sever the heads
of the drake." Well,
you have a Flame
Sword. But what's a
drake?

Go north to the big structure. Look up to see a two-headed
drake at the top.

THE DRAKE TOWER

Climb the tower with your rope-and-hook.

At the top, arm yourself with the Flame Sword. No other
weapon is effective against the drake.

Save your game here!

Hop up the small ledge and attack the drake. You must chop off
both heads with the Flame Sword. Good luck.

After defeating the drake, hop down the hole behind its carcass.

Walk down the tunnel.

You are asked if you want to access a new region. If you have the
Mask piece from the Ice Lord's tower, select Yes. The game loads a
new area called "Paradise Lost."

Figure 6-17
One Down, One to Go. Hack off both heads of the drake with your Flame Sword.

PARADISE LOST

Beautiful, isn't it? Go to the altar in the middle of the Stonehenge-like structure.

Click on the altar. Connor notices a "small depression" on top.

Figure 6-18
Paradise Lost. This area provides a brief respite and passage to the Realm of the Sun, the *sanctum sanctorum* of the Mask of Eternity.

Put the crystal pyramid in the small depression atop the altar. An archon appears. If you have all four of the Mask pieces available at this point, the archon transports Connor to the Realm of the Sun.

CHAPTER 7

Realm of the Sun

here's no turning back now.

You won't find any teleporters in the Realm of the Sun. You can't get in or out of this rarefied place without friends (or enemies) in high places. But don't worry. If the archon transported you here, you have everything you need to finish your quest.

The Temple of the Sun has three levels, each dealing with a single aspect of the Mask of Eternity. At the end lies the Altar Room, the inner sanctum of the Mask. Guess who waits for you there?

TEMPLE LEVEL 1: *TRUTH*

Water Room (Mask Medallion)

- Exit your arrival room and go left (south).

- Ready your weapon and enter the room full of water.

- Kill the Water Snake. Beware her tongue!

See the spot where water drips from above? This is a clue. If you look up to seek the source of the drip, you find an opening in the ceiling. Approach the wall; your rope-and-hook icon appears. Aha! Time to climb.

- Climb the far wall of the water room.

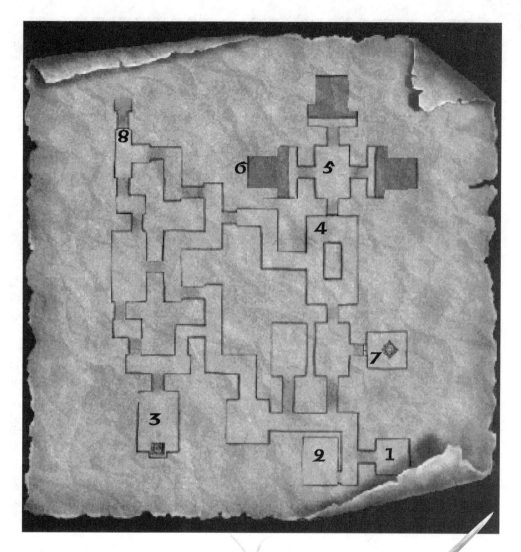

1. Start Level 1
2. Water Room
   (Medallion)
3. Tablet of Knowledge
4. Archon

5. Hall of Truth
6. Key of Truth
7. Sword of Truth
8. Passage to Level 2

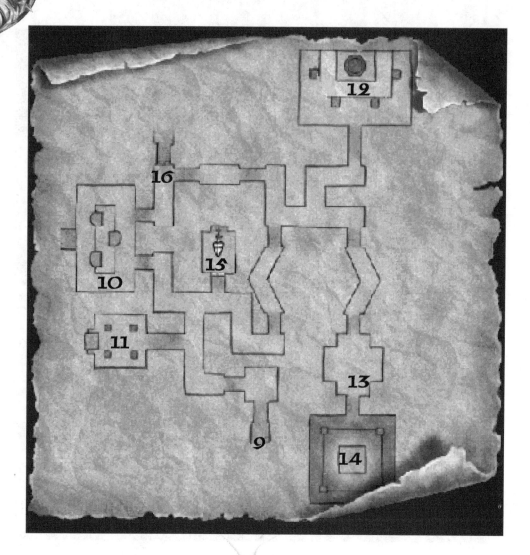

9. Start Level 2
10. Switch (Unlit Candle)
11. Mask Room
12. Cauldron

13. Archon
14. Hall of Light (Key)
15. Armor of Light
16. Passage to Level 3

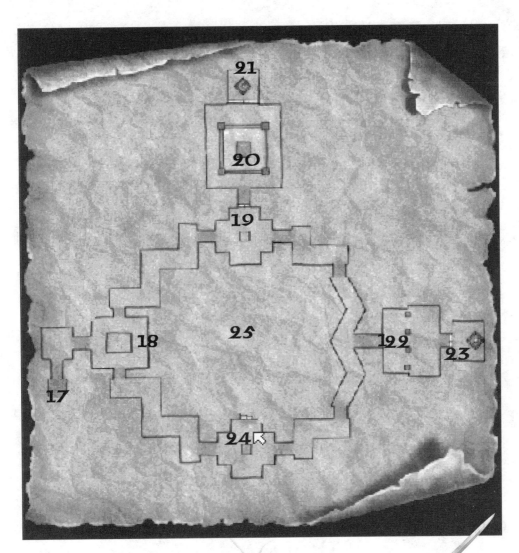

17. Start Level 3
18. Gold Urn (Opens
    Wall Panel)
19. Archon
20. Hall of Order (Mask
    Puzzle)
21. Key of Order
22. Monster Swarm!
23. Chalice of Order
24. Outer Sanctum
    Door
25. Altar Room

Figure 7-1
Mask Medallion.
Climb the water
room wall to that
ceiling niche in the
corner; then snag
the Mask Medallion.

- At the top, break the urn.

- Take the Mask Medallion.

- Climb back down. Watch for a Shadow Demon when you reach bottom.

- Exit the room and turn left (north). Prepare to face hordes of Lucreto's Henchmen and other beasts roaming the hallways.

note Break every urn you see. Most hold health items and/or potions.

SOUTHERN HALLWAYS

- Go north from the water room.

- Take the first left and go west all the way to the room at the end of the hall. Two bloodthirsty Henchman await you.

After dealing with the Henchmen, open secret panels in the south and west walls to get potions.

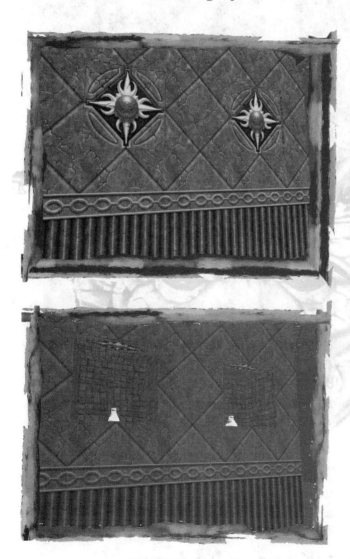

Figure 7-2
Good Panels. On all three levels of the temple, click on any wall panel with the icon shown here. Many cover secret compartments holding valuable potions.

Figure 7-3 **Bad Panels.** When you step on these square floor panels, you release deadly Shadow Demons.

caution

Several areas of the temple feature floor panels (see Figure 7-3) which, when stepped on, release Shadow Demons. They're barely visible; examine the floor carefully when you enter each new room or hallway. If you're low on health items, simply avoid the panels.

- Exit the room to the north.
- Work your way along the left wall until you get to the room full of what appear to be marble statues. (See 3 on the map.)

Tablet of Knowledge

What a sight. The temple archons are frozen before an altar with a stone tablet. But their thoughts swirl in a furious cacophony around the room.

Figure 7-4
Penny for Your Thoughts. The archons of the temple are frozen in marble, but you can hear their thoughts. Listen carefully for clues.

Take the Tablet of Knowledge from the altar. If you examine it in inventory, Connor notes it is "void of its precepts."

Listen to the swirling thoughts of the archon acolytes. Most of them are listed below:

"The Mask of Eternity holds all power."

"Lucreto hath coveted power."

"Lucreto hath caused the Mask's destruction."

"The Chalice of Order provides the light immortal."

"The Armor of Light can protect against Lucreto."

"Only the Sword of Truth can battle Lucreto."

"Immortal Lucreto cannot be slain."

"The precepts are the keys."

"Seek the Tablet. Regain the missing precepts."

"The precepts have vanished from the Tablet of Knowledge!"

"The Mask must be regained and returned to its altar."

"He has vanished. All is darkness and evil."

"We are imprisoned, we are powerless. Lucreto, he hath betrayed us."

"A foul river of death is here in the Temple."

❖ Now you must work your way to the far northeast corner of this level.

❖ Look for the incorporeal archon floating near a big gold door. (See 4 on the map.)

Figure 7-5
Tabula Rasa. Take the Tablet of Knowledge. Your task: Find its missing precepts.

Hall of Truth

- Open all eight secret panels around the block in the center of the room—eight more potions. Of course, the way Henchmen keep coming at you, you're going to need as many potions as you can get.

- Approach the archon and click on him. He opens the doors to the Hall of Truth and says, "Have faith, O Champion. In Trust is Truth."

- Enter the Hall of Truth.

- Enter the first room on your left.

- Have faith and walk off the ledge directly toward the hovering monster. When you get close, the beast transforms into the Key of Truth. See? "In Trust is Truth."

- Take the Key of Truth.

Figure 7-6
Guardian of Truth.
This archon lets champions like you into the Hall of Truth. He suggests you have faith. I suggest you take his word.

Figure 7-7
Have Faith, O Champion. Walk across air into the teeth of this red monster. Your reward for trusting is the Key of Truth.

If you're curious, you can still try the other two rooms off the main hall. In one, a golden sword hovers at the end of a stone bridge. But, of course, this offers no test of faith. Appropriately, if you cross the bridge, the sword transforms into the very monster you saw in the first room—but this guy's for real.

The other room features another golden sword, but this one hovers in the air. If you have faith and walk toward it, an invisible bridge holds you up. But whenever you get close, the sword disappears. Clearly, walking across a chasm toward a frightening monster offers the ultimate test of faith.

- Exit the Hall of Truth.

- Go due south through the room with the secret panels.

Sword of Truth

- Enter the next room carefully! Three floor panels here release Shadow Demons.

- Find another golden door, this one with a keyhole.

Figure 7-8
Bolt of Truth. Take the Sword and Shield of Truth from the altar and get a precept inscribed in your tablet.

 Use the Key of Truth on the keyhole. The door opens.

 Enter.

 Take the Sword and Shield of Truth from the altar. This triggers an automatic sequence.

A voice booms, "Truth is mighty and shall prevail." This is the Precept of Truth. Connor takes out the Tablet of Knowledge and an unseen force inscribes the precept on the tablet with a bolt of lightning.

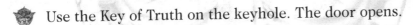 Now work all the way to the northwest corner of the Level 1 map.

On the way, watch for floor panels that release Shadow Demons. Remember, you can avoid them if you find yourself running low on health items and potions.

Figure 7-9
Truth Unsheathed.
Now Truth is on your
side. Plus you've got
some hot new battle
gear.

Door to Level 2

As you step into the corridor and approach the golden door, you hear
a voice ask, "What is the power of Truth?" Given the state of modern
politics, you might be tempted to make cynical remarks. But being
the Champion Eternal, you rise above cynicism. Besides, you have
the answer written in lightning.

- Use the Tablet of Knowledge (inscribed with the Precept of
  Truth) on the door. Connor speaks the precept: "Truth is mighty
  and shall prevail." The door opens!

- Before you go through, be sure to open the secret wall panel
  near the door and grab the potion.

- Now go through the door to the next level.

LEVEL 2: LIGHT

Level 2 is crawling with Lucreto's Henchmen, and for good reason. This is where he manufactures the bloody goons. In general, we suggest you put your Strength and Shield potions to regular use until you figure out a way to shut off the Henchman spigot.

Hidden Switch (Unlit Candle)

- From your starting point in Level 2, follow the left wall until you reach a big room with a center block that has three large urns in alcoves.

- Find the single unlit candle in the room. It's on the south end of the central block. (See 10 on the map.)

- Pull down the unlit candle.

> **note** Don't forget to bash the urns to smithereens and gather the Healing Crystals inside.

Aha! It's a switch that opens a hidden passage elsewhere. Ironic and clever that, in a level devoted to the Precept of Light, the one *unlit* candle is the key to a big secret. But where is this secret? What is the secret? Hey, stop asking questions and follow me.

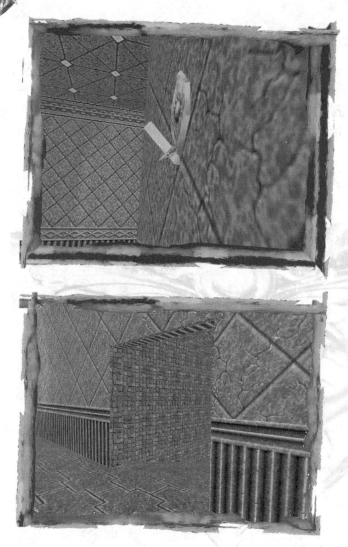

Figure 7-10
Secret Switch. Find the unlit candle and give it a pull. This opens a hidden passage off a nearby hallway.

- Go back the way you came from the starting point, sticking to the right wall.

- Find the newly opened passage in the west wall. (See 11 on the map.)

Hidden Room (Mask Piece)

When you enter the room, you trigger an automatic sequence. Connor finds the fifth and final piece of the Mask of Eternity. But as he leaves the room, he finds two more pike-wielding Henchman blocking his way.

 Defeat the Henchmen.

 Fight your way through roving Henchmen to the big room in the northeast corner of the map. (See 12 on the map.)

Figure 7-11
Last Piece. Connor finds the final Mask piece in the room opened by the unlit candle switch.

Cauldron Room

"Egad! The vision in the witch's cauldron!" When you see a Henchman suddenly emerge from the foul waters of the bubbling basin in this room, you understand what you saw in the Swamp Witch's tower. This thing actually manufactures Henchmen.

Figure 7-12
Bad Guy Soup.
Lucreto's cauldron
spits out Henchmen.
Use the Mask
Medallion to stop the
vile process.

- Use the Mask Medallion (from the water room in Level 1) on the cauldron. It transforms into a sacred healing well.

- Drink as much as you want. Each sip restores health if your rating is down.

- Exit the room and work your way south to another archon outside a golden door.

Hall of Light

- Click on the archon, who opens the door to let you into the Hall of Light. This archon says, "Thou shalt not walk in darkness, but shalt have the light of knowledge."

- Enter the Hall of Light.

- Push the book pedestal to the center of the circle of light. The Key of Light appears.

Figure 7-13
In a Good Light. If you crave enlightenment, push that book pedestal into the center of the circle.

Figure 7-14
Key Discovery. When light hits the book, the Key of Light appears.

 Take the Key of Light.

 Exit the hall.

 Head for the middle of the level to another golden door with a keyhole. (See 15 on the map.)

Armor of Light

- Use the Key of Light to unlock the golden door.

- Enter and take the Armor of Light. Connor dons it and, yes, he's looking pretty darn slick.

- This time the voice says, "A mind enlightened gains the Light of Life." The lightning bolt inscribes the precept on the Tablet of Knowledge.

Figure 7-15
Armor of Light.
The Hall of Light gives you some powerful armor and a second precept for your tablet.

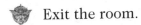 Exit the room.

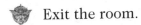 Work your way north and west to the exit door.

Door to Level 3

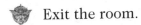 When you approach the door, it asks, "How gainest thou the Light?"

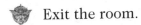 Use the Tablet of Knowledge (now inscribed with the Precept of Light) on the door. Connor speaks the precept: "A mind enlightened gains the Light of Life." The door opens.

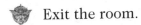 Before you go through, be sure to open the secret panel near the door and grab the potion.

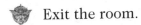 Now go through the door to the next level.

LEVEL 3: ORDER

Your quest is almost complete now. This third level of the temple is remarkably devoid of roaming monsters. But don't worry, brutal tests of combat still lie ahead. As you might guess, you're heading for a showdown with the big boss himself, Lucreto.

Start

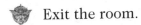 From your starting position, walk around the corner into a large room with a center block.

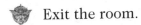 Push the golden urn on the west side of the block. (See 18 on the map.) A wall panel opens nearby, revealing a secret compartment.

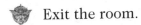 Take the potion from the secret compartment.

 Work your way north and west to the archon at the golden door.

Figure 7-16
Urned Potion. Push
the golden urn to open
a secret compartment.

Hall of Order

 Click on the archon, who opens the hall door, saying: "He who does not control small faults shalt not control great ones."

Enter the Hall of Order.

Push the large golden blocks to form an image of the Mask of Eternity. Doors open on the far side of the hall.

Tip For quick reference, move your game cursor to the top of the screen to see your inventory bar. The Mask icon at far left shows what your block puzzle should look like when successfully assembled.

Figure 7-17
Mask Block Puzzle.
Push the blocks to
form this picture of
the Mask.

- Enter the now-open room to the north.

- Take the Key of Order from the altar.

- Exit the Hall of Order.

- Arm yourself. Monsters hunker in wait at your next destination.

- Work your way south and east to the big room full of bad guys.

Chalice of Order

Two Zombies, two Skeleton Archers, and a very, very tough Commander Skeleton guard the golden door in this room. This is not an easy fight. Keep an eye on your Health rating and quaff as many potions as it takes to stay alive.

Figure 7-18
Need Tutoring. These fellows believe Order should be subjugated to the forces of Chaos. Disabuse them of this horribly misguided notion.

- Consider saving your game before this fight.

- Drink potions of Strength and Shield.

- Wipe out Lucreto's occupation force. Good luck.

- Use the Key of Order to unlock the golden door.

- Enter the back room and take the Chalice of Order from the altar.

The booming voice proclaims, "Order is Unity and therefore Perfect Harmony." Again, this precept is inscribed on your Tablet of Knowledge. Your tablet is now full. Do you sense a grand finale coming on?

- Exit to the corridor.

- Work your way south and west to the golden door that demands, "Speak thou of Order."

Door to the Altar Room

🛡 Use the Tablet of Knowledge on the golden door. Connor speaks the Precept of Order and the door opens.

🛡 Enter the passage. The final level loads.

ALTAR ROOM

Get ready. This is it. If you arrive here with all five pieces of the Mask of Eternity, your showdown with Lucreto is about to begin. And when the going gets tough, just remember: You're the Champion Eternal, he's not.

By the way, if you're low on health items, I highly recommend you scour all three levels of the temple—breaking urns, opening wall panels, and so on—in search of every bit of health-enhancing substance you can find.

You'll need it. Lucreto wields a *mean* staff.

🛡 Click on the floating archon by the door. If you have everything you need, he lets you in. There is no turning back once you enter!

🛡 Step into the Altar Room.

🛡 After your pleasant little exchange with Lucreto, approach the altar. Note that Lucreto's fire attack leaves your health depleted.

🛡 Use health items to bring your Health rating back to 100 percent.

🛡 Take a piece of the Mask from inventory and place it on the altar.

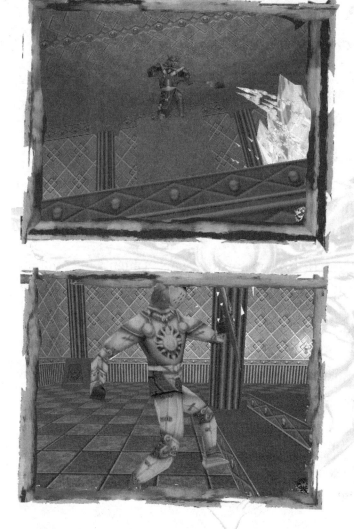

Figure 7-19
You're Getting
Warm. Very, very
warm. Lucreto's
staff spews fire
bolts. Fortunately,
that Shield of Truth
and Armor of Light
keep you from
being charbroiled.

Lucreto finds this action threatening and reappears with a vengeance. Even with the Sword of Truth, the Armor of Light, and the Chalice of Order, you take a serious beating. Remember the audible thoughts of the archons: "Immortal Lucreto cannot be slain."

 Fight Lucreto until he disappears.

Place a second piece of the Mask on the altar. Lucreto reappears.

Fight off Lucreto again.

Place a third piece of the Mask on the altar. Lucreto reappears.

Fight off Lucreto again.

Place a fourth piece of the Mask on the altar. A break! Lucreto makes no appearance this time. Say, do you suppose he's gone forever? If so, please contact me immediately. I'm lining up investors for a real estate venture down in Ecuador.

Place the fifth and final piece of the Mask on the altar. A vortex appears on the back wall. *Keep your distance!* The vortex will suck you right into oblivion.

Figure 7-20
One Way Out. When you place the final Mask piece on the altar, a brilliant vortex opens. Drive the immortal Lucreto into the swirl.

 Engage in your final combat with Lucreto. You must drive him into the vortex.

 Congratulations! You just beat one tough game.

Index

INDEX

INDEX

INDEX